SMART
WEAPONS

SMART
WEAPONS

TOP SECRET HISTORY OF REMOTE
CONTROLLED AIRBORNE WEAPONS

Hugh McDaid and David Oliver

BARNES
&NOBLE
BOOKS
NEW YORK

This edition published by
Barnes & Noble, Inc.,
by arrangement with
The Orion Publishing Group
1997 Barnes & Noble Books

M 10 9 8 7 6 5 4 3 2 1

ISBN 0-7607-0760-X

Printed and bound in Italy

CONTENTS

FOREWORD

**Rear Admiral Barton D. Strong,
Head of the Joint Projects
Office for Cruise Missiles and Unmanned Aircraft,
US Department of Defense**

This is the first general book to cover the past, present and perhaps the future of an increasingly important class of aircraft, namely the Unmanned or Uninhabited Aerial Vehicle. Whatever they may be called in future years, we will see more and more military, as well as commercial, roles performed by these pilotless craft.

The US Armed Forces have traditionally used UAVs in intelligence gathering missions. The first successes came with the Teledyne Ryan Firebees during the Vietnam conflict. Predator, which has been handed over to the USAF following a highly successful ACTD, is currently providing a vital resource to Allied efforts in Bosnia. Outrider, Global Hawk and DarkStar are on the near horizon. Advances are in hand to maximize the ability of sensors, and an efficient and effective distribution architecture will send imagery and intelligence data to the warfighter on demand. What the future holds is open to debate but there no longer is any doubt that UAVs will play a major military role whether it be in open conflict or peacekeeping. UAVs have rapidly gained the attention of military commanders for good reasons. They are relatively inexpensive and can effectively accomplish vital missions without risking human life. We already have sufficient experience with UAVs to know that they will revolutionize warfare.

The number of nations pursuing their own unmanned programmes is rapidly increasing. Israel and South Africa have already used them in conflicts. The French have deployed UAVs in Desert Storm and in Bosnia, while the Canadians also have a history of use and innovation. Other countries such as India, Egypt, Turkey and Sweden are also joining the UAV fraternity.

INTRODUCTION

**Major General Kenneth R. Israel,
United States Air Force Director,
Defense Airborne Reconnaissance Office (DARO),
The Pentagon, Washington, DC**

My first experience with Unmanned Aerial Vehicles (UAVs) was during my service in Vietnam. As an electronic warfare officer in a B-52, I received intelligence information from UAVs which would tell me the exact radar frequency of numerous surface-to-air missile sites. The information allowed me to jam tracking signals and protect my air-craft. The key premise is this: UAVs save lives. They not only supply intelligence, but take the pilot out of high risk situations. We've seen this in Bosnia. When F-16 pilot Captain Scott O'Grady was shot down, it was a crisis, but when a $2-million Predator UAV was shot down, it was a curiosity. Who is going to tell a parent that their child is not worth $2 million?

The family of UAVs under development can do more than take pilots out of harm's way — they offer new revolutionary capabilities to the warfighter. Our tactical UAVs are smaller and more deployable than traditional manned aircraft, allowing troops in the field to see over the next hill, to test the environment for nuclear, chemical or biological threats, or to designate targets for rapid strike by precision-guided munitions. Endurance UAVs will dwell for long periods over an area of interest, revisiting critical targets as often as required, unconstrained by crew-fatigue concerns. These aircraft will provide services that previously could only be performed by satellites. Rapidly deployed high-altitude endurance UAVs will serve as 'surrogate satellites' and relay battlefield communications in addition to gathering intelligence for the warfighter.

We are at a crossroads in the development of uninhabited aircraft. Recent successes by systems such as Pioneer in Desert Storm or Predator in Bosnia have shown the warfighter the military utility of UAVs for surveillance and reconnaissance, particularly in conjunction with the manned systems we relied upon for years. Whatever we call them — drones, remotely pilot-ed vehicles, or UAVs — it is clear that they will play an increasingly important role in many military missions beyond intelligence, surveillance and reconnaissance.

This book offers an historical overview of unmanned aircraft, from the first steps with a gyroscope and the gears and springs of a clock, to the recent roll-out of the Global Hawk high-altitude endurance UAV.

Current and future capabilities described in this work are not science fiction, although there is some speculation by the authors on unsubstantiated activities at clandestine military facilities. Nevertheless, the technologies required for the future of UAVs are here today. The Defense Airborne Reconnaissance Office is working carefully on the entire UAV system — the architecture that integrates airframes, structures, propulsion, avionics, computers and sensors — to vastly increase the utility of UAVs. We have come a long way since Dr Langley's flight over the Potomac River over 100 years ago, but we have only scratched the surface of the potential offered by these robot warriors.

The first heavier-than-air, powered, sustained, controlled flight was achieved by a pilotless aircraft named 'Aerodrome No. 5'. Built by Dr Samuel Pierpoint Langley, he launched his steam-powered craft over the Potomac river on 6 May 1896 for a flight lasting over one minute. It might, therefore, be safely said that unmanned aeroplanes are not a new idea.

In Germany Carl Jatho flew an 11 ft 10 in long

was the invention of the automatic gyroscopic stabilizer (which helps to keep an aircraft flying straight and level) by the Americans Dr Peter Cooper and Elmer A. Sperry, with Lt Patrick Nelson Lynch Bellinger. They carried out limited tests with the first radio-controlled 'aerial torpedoes' at Long Island in December 1917. The converted US Navy Curtiss N-9 trainers were powered by a 40 hp engine and capable of flying 50 miles carrying a 300 lb bomb load.

E a r

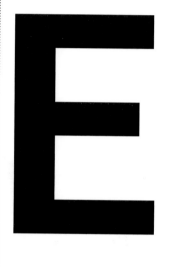

pilotless biplane, powered by a 9.5 hp petrol engine, over a distance of 196 ft at a height of 11 ft in September 1903, further and earlier than the Wright brothers.

UAVs were even flown in World War One. The breakthrough in technology

A more sophisticated unmanned aircraft was designed by Charles F. Kettering of Delco, later General Motors. Powered by a 40 hp Ford engine, the 12 ft wing-span biplane could carry a bomb load equal to its own weight – 300 lb. Built primarily of wood and canvas, the 'Kettering Bug' cost some $400 each and was the first UAV to be mass produced.

Launched from a wheeled trolley, the Bug could be pre-programmed to drop on targets by means of a engine-driven cam which would 'unscrew' the wing-retaining bolts over a set distance. The wings would then 'fold up' and the

Bug would dive vertically towards its target. Although initial tests were somewhat erratic, the Bug was ordered in large quantities in the last months of World War One, although most were cancelled after the armistice.

In Britain in 1916 H. P. Folland and Professor A. M. Low developed their own 'aerial torpedo', a small monoplane, at the Royal Aircraft Establishment (RAE) at Farnborough under the cover name of AT (Aerial Targets). However,

The DH.82B Queen Bee, designed as a target for anti-aircraft gunners, was first flown in January 1935. This spruce-and-plywood biplane drone, powered by a 130 hp Gypsy Major engine, was produced with either wheels, for conventional operation from an airfield, or floats for use at sea, when it was 'fired' from a ship's steam catapult and landed on the sea. The Queen Bee had a ceiling of 17,000 ft and a maximum range of 300 miles at a speed of little over 100 mph. Initially

HISTORY

pilotless-aircraft development almost ceased at the end of the war and it was not seriously revived until 1924, when the RAE built a full-size, Rolls-Royce Lynx-powered, monoplane 'long-range gun' named the Larynx. This was followed in 1931 by the modification of three Fairey IIIF float planes into Fairey Queen radio-controlled targets.

Following Fairey Queen trials with the fleet off Gibraltar, when Royal Navy gunners failed to register a single hit on the drones, the British Air Ministry issued a requirement for a dedicated radio-controlled target aircraft which resulted in a drone variant of the RAF's Tiger Moth basic trainer.

built in small numbers before the outbreak of World War Two, a total of 380 were to serve with the RAF and Royal Navy in the British Isles and overseas until 1947. This is how Bill Young, a wartime pilot/operator, described his time working with the Queen Bee:

In May 1938 I was posted to No. 1 Anti-Aircraft Co-operation Unit [1 AACU] at RAF Cleave, a grass strip on a Cornish cliff near Bude. RAF Cleave claimed to be the first unit to fly an operational Queen Bee, land to land, in the British Isles.

Providing the angle of climb and gliding speeds were set correctly for that particular day's wind speeds, actual or predicted, the take-offs and approaches were no problem. However, the landing was initiated by a weighted trailing aerial which, on contact with the sea or ground, pulled the stick back in two distinct movements and cut the power. Consequently, once the landing sequence started there was no 'going around again'.

Sometimes the Army would put the radio controls out of action with a near hit and then the 'automatic pilot' was designed to put the aircraft into a left-hand glide and close the throttle.

Equally, if for any reason no signal was received from the ground after a certain time, it did

the same manoeuvre. On these occasions there was the inevitable phone call from a farmer who reported a plane crash but was worried because he could not find the pilot.

The aircraft and their radio controls were flight tested with a pilot on board. I remember on several occasions being taken aloft, flown around and put on to the final approach by remote control, but I took over manually for a landing, having seen too many Queen Bees slew across the airfield and end up on their noses.

The Queen Bee was planned to be replaced in RAF and Royal Navy service by the unmanned Airspeed Queen Wasp, the first of which flew in

The world's first offensive UAV, the Kettering Bug, being mass-produced at the end of World War One.

1937. Although it had a maximum speed of 170 mph and could fly at over 20,000 ft, the Queen Wasp was considerably more expensive to build and operate than the simple Queen Bee. Only five production aircraft, powered by a 380 hp Cheetah radial engine, were subsequently delivered to the RAF's No. 1 AACU, with which they served from 1940 until 1943.

In the USA it was the navy which once again took the lead in radio-controlled aircraft development with Project *Dog* in 1936, under the leadership of Lt-Com. (later Rear-Admiral) Delmar S. Fahrney who had been inspired by Britain's successful pilotless Queen Bee. That year, two Stearman Hammond JR-1 twin-boom, single-seater aircraft were converted at the Naval Air Factory at Philadelphia and flight-tested at Cape May Coast Guard Air Station in November 1937. The first JH-1 was 'flown' by a pilot in a Curtiss TG-2 'mother' aircraft. A pilotless radio-controlled version of the US Navy Curtiss N2C-2 flown at Cape May later that month was the first NOLO (no live operator) flight.

As part of Project *Dog*, the first assault drone was developed by Fahrney, when a pilotless N2C-2 dive-bombed the USS *Utah* in September 1938. However, before the attack took place the N2C was hit by a stray anti-aircraft round fired by an over-anxious gunner in a nearby ship and crashed short of the target. War in Europe had now begun and US Navy funding continued for the development of assault drones, using obsolete aircraft for the purpose of conversion.

In 1939 VJ-3 (Utility Squadron Three) was formed under the command of one of Fahrney's assistants, LTJG Bob Jones, at NAS San Diego to begin operations with target and assault drones.

In April 1941 it was the newly formed VJ-5 based at NAS Cape May which carried out the first live attack with a remotely piloted TG-2, armed with a dummy warhead torpedo, against a manoeuvring destroyer. Controlled by a 'mother' aircraft 20 miles away, the drone released its torpedo and scored a direct hit on the destroyer's target raft.

As a result of this and other successful trials, 500 assault drones, with 170 control aircraft, were

The US Navy's first radio-controlled pilotless aircraft, the Curtiss N2C-2, flew in 1937. (Maxwell White/NAWCWD)

ordered in 1942 under Project *Option*. The Naval Aircraft Factory designed the twin-engined TDN-1 which could carry a torpedo or a 2,000 lb bomb at a cruising speed of 175 mph. In fact, only 164 production TDN-1s were delivered to training units of the US Navy. Its successor, the TDR-1, carried out the first live operations in July 1944, when four drones of STAG-1 (Special Task Air Group One), loaded with 2,000 lb bombs, took off from the northern Solomon Islands against a Japanese merchantman, the *Yamazuki Maru*, and scored two direct hits. STAG-1 launched a total of 46 TDR-1s from Banika Island, near Guadalcanal, between September and October 1944, achieving a 50 per cent hit rate.

The Naval Aircraft
Factory TDR-1 unmanned
attack aircraft was used in
combat in the Pacific
theatre in 1944. (Maxwell
White/NAWCWD)

However, it was Germany which first built a dedicated robot 'flying bomb' with pre-programmed guidance – the V-1 Doodlebug.

HOLLYWOOD – THE GLAMOROUS YEARS

Even the few people who know a little about the early history of the unmanned aircraft would not naturally associate it with Hollywood in the glamorous years of the 1930s and 1940s, but that is exactly where and when some of the most important developments took place. Although many individuals played a part in the story of unmanned aircraft, two stand out.

The first was an actor who appeared in many of the early talkie film hits, including *Anna Karenina* with Greta Garbo and *Mr Blandings Builds His Dream House* with Cary Grant and Myrna Loy. His stage name was Reginald Denny (Reginald Leigh Daymore). Although from a theatrical family, Denny was fascinated by flying, which led him to join the Royal Flying Corps (RFC) in 1917 as an aerial gunner. After demobbing he made his way to Hollywood and started his career as a film actor. However, his interest in aviation also led him to open a model-aeroplane shop in Hollywood Boulevard in the early 1930s. With a growing interest in electronics, Denny hired a number of radio hams and engineers and together they set to work on what was in reality a large, remote-controlled model aeroplane. Radioplanes was officially formed in 1939, with many of its early employees being poached from the neighbouring Lockheed company. The organization's first real success came in 1941 with the model OQ-2A Target which the US Army Air Force ordered in substantial numbers – over 3,800. The facility to manufacture such numbers was

Norma Jean Dougherty, better known as Marilyn Monroe, worked in the Radioplane factory during World War Two, assembling the OQ-3. (Northrop Grumman)

established in a building next to what is now Van Nuys Airport. Radioplanes and its successor, Northrop (now Northrop/Grumman), would go on to build over 72,000 unmanned aircraft in the ensuing years.

The OQ-2, which went by the US Navy designation TDD-1 ((Target Drone Denny), was an extremely simple and elegant design for the time. It was powered by a two-cylinder engine which drove contra-rotating propellers. This reduced the effect of twisting, or torque, which was produced as the engine was speeded up. Its fuel tank held just a gallon and a half of petrol and it could fly for nearly an hour at about 85 mph. The radio-control equipment was manufactured by a young company called Bendix (which still makes hi-tech avionics). The take-off technique was 'compared to that of a slingshot', with winch-stretched rubber bands providing the impetus. Recovery was by means of a 24-foot parachute. Most of the breakable parts were interchangeable and quickly repaired.

The OQ-3 followed in 1943. It was heavier and slightly faster and it was superseded by the OQ-14 which took the speed up to a heady 140 mph.

These vehicles, of which over 10,000 were built, were used to train a whole generation of US Army and Navy anti-aircraft gunners at a cost of about $600 apiece. This modest aircraft helped to form the basis of an aviation dynasty which has remained with us to the present day.

The other notable person in the Radioplane story is a woman; but not just any woman, for she was and remains one of the best-recognized females of the twentieth century. Her name at the time was Norma Jean Dougherty, better known as Marilyn Monroe! Having arrived in California, Norma Jean managed to get a job at Radioplane as an assembler on the OQ-3 production line. Her rise to fame might be said to have properly begun on 26 June 1945, when a photographer was sent to Radioplane by his commanding officer, one Captain Ronald Reagan (an acting buddy of Denny's), to photograph women war workers. The camera and the photographer loved Norma Jean and he persuaded her to model for more photos which soon were circulating in Hollywood. A screen test, a change of name and a career very different from assembling robot planes quickly followed. The rest, as they say, is history …

WORLD WAR TWO – THE BEGINNINGS OF REMOTE WARFARE

The Fieseler Fi-103, better known as the V-1, was ordered at Hitler's behest specifically for use against 'non-military targets'. Its unique throbbing or buzzing sound was produced by a pulse-jet. This was a type of propulsion first proposed during World War One by a French artillery officer, René Lorin, as the power source for an 'unmanned' aircraft and developed by Germany's Argus Motorenwerke in the 1930s.

Project *Kirschkern* (cherry-stone) was the code-name for the 670 lb thrust Argus pulse-jet powered flying bomb that could carry a 2,000 lb warhead. Designed by Fieseler Flugzeughau of Kassel to fly at 470 mph and to be launched from a 230-foot log ramp, the first prototype was in fact air-launched from under the wing of a Focke-Wulf Fw-200 bomber at Peenemunde in December 1942.

The Luftwaffe-operated Fieseler Fi-103, *Vergeltungswaffe* (revenge weapon)-1, was first successfully ground-launched in December 1943 by *Flak Regiment* 155 from sites in the Pas de Calais. At least 13,000 V-1s were built and 5,823 of the 8,564 V-1s, code-named *Divers* launched against Britain, the first on 13 June 1944. They killed more than 900 civilians and injured over 35,000. Eleven Air Defence of Great Britain (ADGB) squadrons were deployed by the RAF to combat the V-1. RAF bombers dropped a total of 16,000 tons of bombs on V-1 sites, known as *Noballs*, in France. To compensate for the loss of V-1 ground-launch sites, the *Luftwaffe's* KG-53 operated over 100 Heinkels He-111s for air-launching a single V-1 from under the port wing, between the engine and the fuselage. To avoid British air defences, the German crew had to operate their outdated and overloaded Heinkels at night and at low level. They flew over the English Channel at 300 ft, below British radar, and 'popped up' to 1,500 ft some 40 miles from the targets to launch the flying bombs. Some 1,200 V-1s were air-launched up to 14 January 1945, but less than half that number crossed the English coast and only one in ten arrived at their target.

As part of Operation *Crossbow*, which was controlled from RAF Biggin Hill, RAF fighters destroyed 1,771 V-1s before they reached their

V1

Germany's V-1 Revenge weapon was the first unmanned flying bomb to be successfully used to attack Britain during World War Two. The Fieseler Fi-103, later designated the FZG-76, or 'long-range target apparatus' was powered by 670 lb thrust pulse jet, the V-1, nicknamed 'Doodlebug' or 'Buzz-Bomb' by the British, was launched from 250 ft long ramps built along the French and Belgian coasts.

Carrying a 2,000 lb explosive warhead, the V-1 cruised at over 400 mph and was pre-programmed to fly between 100 and 150 miles before the engine cut out and it dropped on its target. 5,823 V-1s that fell on Britain killed almost 1,000 people in major British cities. The innovative V-1 was used to develop America's post-war missile and UAV programmes.

Two captured Fieseler Fi-103 V-1s; the one in the foreground is mounted on its launch ramp. They were powered by a simple Argus Rohr (Tube) pulse-jet. (A.P. Bishop)

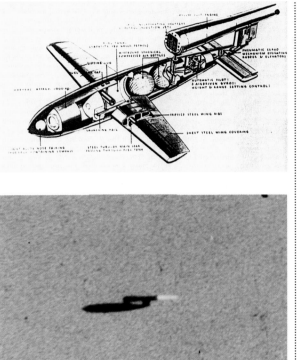

The German pulse-jet powered V-1 Doodlebug, or Buzz Bomb seen flying over England in 1944. The unmanned flying bomb killed more than 900 people in six months. (National Archives)

targets. The most successful RAF unit in the battle against the V-1 was 150 Wing based at Newchurch, near Dungeness in Kent. Two of the Wing's three squadrons were equipped with the 435 mph Hawker Tempest V, whose four 20 mm cannon claimed 638 V-1s, more than any other aircraft type.

150 Wing was led by Wing Commander Roland Beaumont, later English Electric's chief test pilot. His recommendations to the Senior Air Staff of 11 Group, which controlled his Wing's sector, were instrumental in the success of Operation Crossbow. His report read:

Fighter patrols should be concentrated between Eastbourne and Dover in a belt extending 7,000 ft high and three miles out to sea. Within that operational area, guns (AAA) should be restricted from firing, and all slow fighters should be withdrawn, leaving the field clear for the Tempests, some squadrons of special Spitfires, and Mustangs with increased boost. Observer Corps posts should be concentrated at half-mile intervals and equipped with rockets to be fired towards the position of the V-1 reported on the radar plot. The converging rockets should help the patrolling fighter to sight the target quickly.

To combat the V-1 threat further, drone versions of US bombers were developed in July 1944 as part of the USAAF/Navy Project *Anvil*, based at Fersfield, England. The US Navy's SAU-1 (Special Air Unit One) used PB4Y-1 Liberators equipped with remote control, a TV-guidance system, and

America's most successful World War Two target drone was the simple Radioplane OQ-2 built by World War One flyer, and Hollywood actor, Reginald Denny. (David Oliver)

loaded with 25,000 lb of torpex high explosive. Guided by a PV-1 Ventura 'mother' aircraft, the PB4Y-1 would take off with a two-man crew who would climb to 2,000 ft and set a course for V-1 sites in France before bailing out. However, the first Anvil operation by SAU-1, on 12 August 1944, was a tragic failure. Flown by a volunteer crew of Lt Joseph Kennedy Jr, brother of the future US President, John F. Kennedy, and Lt Bud Willy, PB4Y-1 Bureau Number 32271 exploded soon after take-off and before the crew's planned bale-out over the English Channel. Despite this failure, a PB4Y-1 drone was used successfully against German submarine pens on Heligoland Island.

Twenty-five USAAF B-17s were converted in a similar way as part of Project Aphrodite and they also flew from Fersfield. Some of the drones, known as BQ-7s, had open cockpits to enable the crew to bale out more easily. These converted US bombers were the first unmanned aircraft in history to be used against unmanned flying bombs.

Following the rising losses of V-1 launch sites and the lack of success by air-launched V-1s, a secret project, code-named *Reichenberg*, was put into operation in May 1944: the construction of piloted V-1 'suicide' bombers. (In the event, Germany's V-1 mounted 'suicide group' never went into action.)

The first piloted version of the V-1 featured a cockpit directly behind the wing, an auxiliary power unit, landing flaps and landing skids. It was built within a week and one of the first people to flight-test it was the renowned German test pilot, Hanna Reitsch:

On one occasion, the pilot of the He-III had just released me from beneath the bomber's wing when his plane grazed the rear of the V-1. There was a loud noise, as if the tail of my plane had been broken right off. Though only just able to continue to control the plane, I managed to make a smooth landing, finding when I inspected it, that the tail had been crumpled and twisted to the right through an angle of almost thirty degrees. It seemed a miracle that it had not come right off!

On another occasion, I was testing the behaviour of the two-seat model of the V-1 at a wide range of speed along an inclined flight-path, flying at speeds of up to 530 mph. During the test, a sack of sand, which had been wedged in the front seat, on my instructions, to supply extra weight, somehow broke loose and shifted position. In blissful ignorance, I tried to flatten out at speed and suddenly found that I could not move the elevator. I had not enough height, or time, to be able to bale out by parachute and had to risk all on a last faint chance of saving myself and the plane. Just before the machine reached the ground, I pushed her nose down and then, with all the response I could get out of the elevator, quickly pulled out again. This manoeuvre checked the plane just enough for me to be able to make a landing, though an extremely hard one which splintered the skids and the hull. I emerged without a scratch …

In addition to Operation Aphrodite, British-based B-17s of 303 Bomb Group also dropped TV-guided Aeronca GB-1 glider bombs on Cologne in May 1944 without any positive results. Germany had also developed a series of radio-controlled glider bombs, including the FZG-76, the Henshel Hs-293 and the PG-400X (Fritz-X). Six Do-217K-2s of III/KG 100 based at Marseilles attacked the Italian fleet with Fritz-Xs in September 1943, which resulted in the sinking of the cruiser *Roma*. In January 1944 a Royal Navy cruiser and a destroyer were also sunk at Anzio by Fritz-Xs. More than 850 FZG-76s were launched against targets in England by Heinkel He-111H bombers of KG 53 based at Venlo, near the Dutch border, in September 1944 during Operation *Rumpel Kammer*. Few reached their targets; those that did caused minimal damage. The more sophisticated Hs-293 was deployed against bridges over the River Oder in March 1945 in an attempt to slow the Allied advance. They were launched from He-111H aircraft of II/KG 200 and guided to the target with a simple joystick controller by a pilot installed in the nose of the launch Heinkel. The four-engined He-177A-3/RB was also adapted as an Hs-293, but they were too few and too late to be effective.

Also used against the Oder bridges in the last days of the war in Europe were *Mistels* (mistletoe), radio-controlled, unmanned Ju-88s laden with 8,500 lb of explosives. They were guided to their targets by piloted Me-109 or Fw-190 fighters mounted on the back of the bomber. Once the combination, code-named project *Beethoven*, had aligned on the target, the fighter pilot released the Ju-88, which continued on to impact under the control of its automatic pilot. Over 100 *Mistels* were built before the end of the war. They were put to limited use during the Allied D-Day landings with aircraft operated by IV/KG 101 from St Dizier. The *Mistel* attacks hit four of the Oder bridges as part of Operation *Eisenhammer* (iron hammer). The *Mistels* were from II/KG 200 based at Rechlin Larz, which was bombed out of existence by the USAAF in April 1945.

A German Mistel 2 flying bomb composite at Merseburg. The unmanned lower component was a Ju-88G bomber packed with explosives that was flown to its target area by the manned Fw-190A fighter mounted above it.

A sequence showing a Japanese Baka (Fool) flying bomb being released from a Mitsubishi G4M-2 Betty bomber on its one-way mission in June 1945. (National Archives)

On the other side of the world, Japan was launching its own version of the V-1 against US Navy task forces positioned in the Pacific. The Yokosuka MXY-8 *Ohka* (meaning cherry blossom; the Allied code-name is *Baka*, Japanese for fool) was carried under the wing of a Mitsubishi G4M-2 Betty of the 721st Kokutai, which attacked US Task Force FV58 on 21 March 1945. The Bettys were intercepted by US Navy fighters and were forced to release the drone bombs short of their targets. As a result, none of the targets were hit. A week later the USS *Virginia* was damaged by an *Ohka*, but this was the last successful attack by a Japanese drone. In April 1945 US Navy VPB-109 PB4Y-1 Privateers launched remotely guided SWOD-9 BAT bombs against the Japanese

shipping in Balikpapau harbour, Borneo. At almost the same time ten Mitsubishi Ki.67 Type 4 *Hiryu* bombers were used to launch 1,760 lb, guided, Mitsubishi I-Go-1A bombs six miles from their targets – US shipping.

At the end of World War Two the US Navy flight-tested a modified version of the captured German V-1 called the Loon, and 12 former German V-1 specialists were sent to the US Navy's Pilotless Aircraft Unit at Point Mugu, California, in 1947 as part of Operation Paperclip. Target drones developed at Point Mugu in the 1950s included pilotless versions of the F6F Hellcat and F9F Panther fighters, and the P2V

A US Navy PB4Y Privateer converted to an unmanned target drone at Point Mugu. Earlier versions were used in World War Two to destroy V-1 sites in Europe as part of Operation *Anvil*. (Maxwell White/ NAWCWD)

Neptune and PB4Y Privateer patrol bombers. One of the first tasks for the F6F-3K drones was to monitor air samples during Operation Crossroads, the US atomic bomb tests in 1946/7. With the start of the Korean War, Capt. Bob Jones was again tasked with providing the US Navy with a practical combat drone. GMU-90 (Guided Missile Unit 90) was established at NAS San Diego in July 1952, equipped with F6F-5K Hellcats. By August 1952, six F6F-5Ks and two AD-2Q Skyraider control aircraft were embarked on the carrier USS *Boxer en route* for Korea.

The six Hellcat drones, each carrying 2,000 lb GP bombs, were flown against North Korean targets between 28 August and 2 September. Three of the GMU-90 aircraft scored direct hits against their assigned targets. However, due to political and budgetary constraints, no further assault-drone deployment took place during the course of the Korean War.

Although the F6F-5K continued to carry out useful tasks with the US Navy, including early testing of the AIM-9 Sidewinder air-to-air missile, Point Mugu had begun flight-testing the Regulas guided missile and two of the most important US Navy projects of this era: the small propeller-driven, catapult-launched KD4G-1 drone, and the Ryan Firebee.

Ryan Aviation's founder, Claude E. Ryan, had been responsible for building Lindbergh's 'Spirit of St Louis'. The company had been a manufacturer primarily of trainer aircraft during World War Two, but having garnered information on Nazi jet engines and swept wings, it saw the need for a target to emulate the new, faster enemy aircraft. Since 1947 the Firebee has represented one of the most enduring and widely used unmanned aircraft. Over the years other targets have been

aircraft for deployment on all of the US Navy's destroyer fleet by 1963. The contract to supply 900 DASH drones based on the YRON-1 Rotorcycle was awarded to the Gyrodyne Helicopter Company in 1960. The prototype, known as the DSN-1, was powered by a 72 hp Porsche flat-four engine driving two two-bladed coaxial rotors. After a protracted development

ne of EXPLORATION

cheaper and some have been produced in greater numbers, but none has equalled the versatility and adaptability of the basic Firebee design. Not only had it the speed and range to emulate three generations of enemies, but it could carry the heavier and heavier electronic payloads demanded by its customers. Guns, unguided missiles, air-to-air missiles, surface-to-air missiles, even ones with nuclear-tipped warheads, tried to blow the Firebees to oblivion.

One of the most ambitious post-war US Navy drone programmes was the Drone Anti-Submarine Helicopter (DASH). This called for the development of a remotely piloted, rotary-wing

during which a safety pilot was flown in the aircraft, the first production aircraft, designated the QH-50C, took to the air at Patuxent River in January 1962.

A US Navy Radioplane KD4G-1 unmanned target drone on its launch catapult being tested at Point Mugu in 1950. (Maxwell White/NAWCWD)

Powered by a 270 shp Boeing T50-BO-4 turboshaft, the QH-50C was designed to be launched from a destroyer's aft flight deck as soon as contact was made with a target submarine by the ship's sonar. The drone was controlled from the ship's Combat Information Centre (CIC). When the sonar and the DASH's positions coincided, the controller actuated arming and release switches to drop a torpedo or nuclear weapon. The QH-50C was then flown back to the ship and retrieved by an automatic cable-landing system that permitted the drone to operate in any sea condition suitable for anti-submarine operations.

The USAF used many surplus jet fighters as drone targets, such as this QF-86F which was converted by Tracor. (Tracor)

The DASH programme planned for two QH-50Cs, plus one reserve aircraft, on each destroyer. The cost per unit in 1963/4 was $125,000 without guidance system or weapons (one or two Mark 44 or 46 torpedoes or nuclear weapons). Equipment on the destroyers included a small heated hangar and a stern helipad, along with the Landing Assist Device (LAD).

Unfortunately, persistent vibration problems, which caused 26 of the first 100 drones to crash, led to the order for 900 QH-50Cs being reduced to 534 by 1966. However, the Japanese Maritime Self-Defence Force acquired a batch of 16 QH-50Cs in 1968. An improved version, the QH-50D, powered by an uprated engine with glass-fibre blades fitted with a de-icing system, was evaluated by the USAF at Nellis Air Force Base in 1972/3 for its Nite Gazelle programme.

The USAF made extensive use of the Firebee during the Vietnam War; prior to that had experimented with unmanned conversions of heavy bombers for drones. Post-war production of QB-17 target drones was followed in 1960 by the conversion by Lockheed of 14 QB-47E Stratojets and a number of DB-47As as 'mother' aircraft for the unmanned aircraft. However, the project proved costly and was ultimately abandoned, although the USAF subsequently converted large numbers of surplus fighters into target drones. These included the QF-80A, QF-86, QF-100, QF-104A, QF-106 and QF-4.

LOCKHEED D-21 – FASTER, HIGHER, STEALTHIER

The shooting-down of Gary Powers' Lockheed U-2 over central Russia in 1960 was directly responsible for the development of the fastest and highest-flying unmanned aircraft ever to reach operation. The near-impervious curtain of secrecy surrounding this plane, however, makes definitive statements about 'Black' (Special Access Program) projects an uncertain art. In fact, it was only by accident that the D-21 came to light, and this was years after it had been withdrawn from service.

In the wake of the downing of Powers and his U-2 and the subsequent political embarrassment to the US government, the CIA and other US defence services were forbidden by President Eisenhower from overflying Russia or mainland China. Reconnaissance satellites were still in their infancy and appeared overhead in such a predictable

QH-50 DASH

The little known but highly successful US Navy QH-50 Drone Anti-Submarine Helicopter (DASH) is still in use as a test vehicle 25 years after its first deployment on US Navy destroyers.

In 1966, six QH-50s code-named *Snoopy,* carried out extended range surveillance in the Gulf of Tonkin during the Vietnam conflict.

More recently the co-axial rotary-wing UAV has been used to test defensive electronic counter-measures (DECM) which included IR jammers and decoys, and under programme *Nite Gazelle,* carrying bomblet containers, Sidewinder air-to-air missiles and 7.62 mm mini-guns.

Dornier's Do 32U, Geamos and Seamos vertical take-off and recovery UAVs are based on the Gyrodyne QH-50.

Dornier's Seamos technology demonstrator, based on the US Navy QH-50 DASH, being launched from a simulated warship's landing pad. (Dornier)

Below left
The Dornier Seamos coaxial, rotary-wing UAV has been designed to meet NATO's Naval Vertical Take-off and Recovery (VTOR) UAV requirement. (Dornier)

Below far left
The world's first anti-submarine UAV helicopter, the QH-50 DASH, 500 of which were delivered to the US Navy in the 1960s. (Maxwel White/NAWCWD)

The Mach 3.3 D-21 UAV was carried on the back of a Lockheed M-12 'mother' aircraft and had a range of 3,000 miles. Like the M-12, it was a product of the famous Lockheed 'Skunk Works' at Burbank, California. (Lockheed Martin Skunk Works)

manner that they could only see things that were impossible to cover up or hide, such as airfields or nuclear test sites. So, with the Cold War at its height, no money or effort was spared in trying to obtain high-quality images of important targets. Thus Lockheed's 'Skunk Works', under the leadership of the legendary Clarence 'Kelly' Johnson, was given the job of developing a high-

designation of the two aircraft reflected the arrangement: the A-12 becoming the M-12, M standing for mother. The drone element was called D-21, D standing for daughter and the 21 to avoid confusion with A-12 family.

To speed up the design and development stage, the engine from the Bomarc nuclear-tipped surface-to-air missile was used. This proved to be

Powered by a Marquardt RJ43-MA-11 ram-jet, the 43 ft long D-21A had a wing-span of 19 ft. It was fitted with flangible nose- and tail-cones when carried on the M-12. (Lockheed Martin Skunk Works)

speed reconnaissance drone. Having built and tested the 2,000 mph A-12 for the CIA and the SR-71 'Blackbird' for the USAF – which was to have been the manned replacement for the U-2 – Johnson and his small team of designers decided that the best arrangement for such a long-range strategic system was to have the unmanned craft carried to its launch point on the back of the A-12. This had the benefit of making use of an already developed and paid-for manned vehicle, while keeping the unmanned element as small and, therefore, as cheap as possible. The official

highly successful, especially as it could be used while attached to the mothercraft to boost speed and acceleration.

Although at its design speed of 2,000+ mph and operational height of 80,000+ ft the unmanned D-21 was effectively invulnerable to attack, Johnson decided to apply the emerging technology of stealth to the design, as he had with the A-12 (and subsequently with the SR-71). The major structures were covered with an early version of a radar-defeating coating which Johnson enigmatically referred to as 'plastics'. In this respect the D-21 was one of the precursors of the F-117 Stealth Fighter and B-2 Stealth Bomber, as well as another Skunk Works' UAV DarkStar.

With such an advanced project, difficulties inevitably arose. Navigation was a problem. The Honeywell/Kollsman star-tracker system was a 'complete shambles', while the Hycon camera needed modifications to achieve the required

ft and a speed of Mach 3.3. The cost of launching the vehicle was, however, higher than expected and Johnson mused about using a B-52 as the 'mother' and a rocket booster to take the D-21 up to effective operational speed. The success continued with the third flight in June, when the drone flew 1,600 miles and made eight pre-programmed turns.

On 30 July the fourth flight was attempted and

A production D-21B Tagboard, with its solid-fuel booster, suspended on the underwing pylon of a B-52H Stratofortress. (Lockheed Martin Skunk Works)

6-inch ground resolution photography. Aerodynamics were also a serious issue, particularly the all-important release from the mother ship. Eventually it was decided that the best results would come from a separation in a very slight nose-over or dive manoeuvre.

The first flight took place from the 'desert test facility' – the famous Groom Lake airfield in Area 51 – on 5 March 1965. Although the drone was lost after only 150 miles, the event was declared 'a great success'. The second flight followed in April, reaching a range of 1,200 miles, a height of 90,000

brought with it disaster. On release at over 2,000 mph the D-21 pitched up violently and struck the M-12. The crew – pilot Bill Park and launch-system operator Ray Torick – ejected safely into the sea 150 miles off the Californian coast, but by the time the rescue helicopter reached them, Torick had drowned. This event sounded the death knell for the M-12/D-21 combination. However, the B-52 option received funding.

Because the Skunk Works did not have their own B-52 to experiment with, they worked with the 4200 Test Wing at Beale Air Force Base, close

The first of many Ryan UAVs, the Q-2 Firebee, was launched from Holloman Air Force Base, New Mexico, in the spring of 1951. (Teledyne Ryan)

to Sacramento, California. The unit modified two B-52Hs to carry a boosted D-21 under each wing, which was a load of 24 tons. Several failures occurred before the first successful flight took place on 16 June 1968. Over 3,000 miles were covered; a height of 90,000 ft was attained and the photographic package was recovered. A new inertial navigation system was installed, with the code-name 'Captain Hook' which, after a couple of failed attempts, meant that the system was considered operational.

The first operational mission, allegedly over China, took place on 9 November 1969. The aircraft launch was successful, but it then vanished over enemy territory. No reason was ever given for this; however navigation failure was suspected. For various reasons no further operations were attempted until December 1970, when the flight appears to have been a success, even though the recovery of the vital film contained in the ejectable hatch was not achieved. The third hot mission, in March 1971, seems to have been problem-free until the parachute failed. The US Navy was on hand

for the recovery – the hatch was designed to float – but apparently the hatch was accidentally rammed by the recovery ship and it sank without trace. A fourth and final mission was flown on 20 March 1971. Contact was lost with this craft 'over a heavily defended territory'. The project was officially cancelled in July 1971 and the remaining airframes were placed in open storage at the Davis Monthan Air Force Base – the aircraft 'bone yard'. The D-21 never flew again, although there were reports that NASA was planing to use it for high-speed research. Some sources suggested that this was part of a front for the mysterious high-speed project code-named Aurora. Knowledgeable observers have even claimed that the liquid hydrogen-powered Aurora, supposed to be capable of flying at 4,000–6,000 mph, was also unmanned. Maybe in a decade or so we may find that a modern equivalent of the D-21 had been flying equally exotic and mysterious missions.

VIETNAM – THE WONDER YEARS

The most important attribute of unmanned aircraft is not that they are cheaper or more clever than manned aircraft, but they can save pilots' lives. The place they proved this was over Vietnam. Ironically, the first South East Asian unmanned aircraft missions in 1964 were not over Vietnam at all, but over its weapons supplier and co-conspirator, communist China.

This story begins in 1960 when Robert R. Schwanhausser of Ryan Aeronautical (later to become Teledyne Ryan Aeronautical) made a proposal to the USAF to use modified unpiloted target drones for reconnaissance missions. He succeeded in getting an initial $200,000 for a feasibility study which would be code-named *Red Wagon* and then *Lucy Lee*. This was no ordinary study; in fact it was one of the first stealth projects, and therefore extremely secret. It involved reducing the radar signature of a modified Q-2C Firebee target drone by placing a specially designed screen over the engine's air-intake, putting radar-absorbing blankets on the fuselage sides and then covering the whole aircraft with a newly developed anti-radar paint.

The tests proved successful enough to be included in the Big Safari system of acquiring covert and speedy means of getting reconnaissance information without having to go through official 'channels'. The use of these Firebees for reconnaissance was given the code-name *Fire Fly*, which was

were along the coast and interior of southern China. Launched from under the wings of DC-130 Hercules transports flying well inside international airspace, they were recovered by parachute on the friendly island of Taiwan.

The aircraft used on these and subsequent missions were not the highly sophisticated stealth drones but stretched models of the disposable Q-2 target drones. Their wing-span had been widened by 12 ft to give better altitude performance and their fuselage lengthened by some 4 ft to make room for the camera, navigation equipment and extra fuel. How many missions these aircraft flew over China is still secret. However, a total of 78

then changed to Lightning Bug. After the Gulf of Tonkin resolution in October 1964, and under the auspices of the USAF's Strategic Air Command (SAC), the modified drones set out on their first operational mission. Their home was Kadena Air Force Base, Okinawa, in Japan, and their targets

missions were over enemy territory, which from August 1964 to December 1975 included Vietnam. The return rate for these sorties was 61.5 per cent. The Firebees that did not make it home were probably either shot down or crashed through mechanical failure. The pictures that were brought

More than 130 high-altitude, photo-recce Ryan AQM-34N UAVs were flown over North Vietnam between 1967 and 1971.

LIGHTNING BUGS IN VIETNAM

The Ryan Firebee started life as a high performance target drone, but following a feasibility study in 1960, it proved to be one of the most successful surveillance UAVs in history. From October 1964 to April 1975, more than 1,000 Firebees flew over 34,000 operational surveillance missions over Southeast Asia – without the loss of a single pilot

They were deployed from Japan, South Vietnam and Thailand, and flew high- and low-level surveillance, COMMINT and leaflet dropping missions over North Vietnam and south east China. More than 75% of the Firebees returned to fly another day.

A handful were shot down over China which was so impressed by the UAV that it reverse engineered the Firebee and built them in China for nearly 20 years.

A Ryan 147TE Combat Dawn high-altitude, real-time COMINT UAV, fitted with a long-range auxiliary fuel tank, being ferried back to its base by a 'Jolly Green Giant' helicopter in 1973. (Teledyne Ryan)

The wide-span, high-altitude Ryan 147H had a 2,400 mile range. It was first deployed in Vietnam in 1967. This one has been retrieved by a US Navy HH-3, to be flown back to its base for another mission. (Teledyne Ryan)

Vietnamese soldiers rejoice over a crashed Firebee.

A captured Ryan 147 Firebee, named 'Black Beauty', on display at China's Aerospace Museum in Beijing! (David Oliver)

back created a lot of supporters among the reconnaissance community. One of these was a young USAF officer who would go on to command many of the most important UAV missions over Vietnam, Lt. Col. John Dale. Here is his description of the UAVs in that war:

The UAV program during the Vietnam War was a closely held Top Secret 'black' program that started in 1964. Initially, photos of the UAVs, either by themselves or on the wings of their DC-130 launch aircraft, were not allowed. We were not even allowed to call them 'drones', but used the term 'SPA', for Special Purpose Aircraft.

Their first operational use was for the overflight of China at high altitude, with recovery in Taiwan. Next, operational sorties were flown from Bien Hoa Air Base in the Republic of Vietnam, with recovery taking place at Da Nang Air Base [a USMC forward fire base near the ironically named demilitarized zone]. These pioneering UAVs were Ryan Aeronautical Model 147 series aircraft. They were modified Firebee target drones and were funded through 'Big Safari', an Air Force program designed to provide funds for a few reconnaissance vehicles and administered through the Air Force Logistics Command (AFLC) at Wright Patterson Air Force Base. Ryan Aeronautical came up with design changes to the Firebee that increased altitude, range and payload capabilities enabling us to expand the UAVs' missions. By the end of the war we had a high-altitude bird good for over 75,000 feet that could carry a 300 lb camera. Those aircraft equipped with early detection and jamming could walk around SAM sites, manoeuvre and jam against attacking SA-2 missiles, and had unlimited headings to provide programming operations to

thwart MiG attacks. While I had the SPA Branch at Strategic Air Command Headquarters, I never lost a high-altitude sortie to MiGs or SAMs over China or North Vietnam and they sure as hell tried!

All of these missions were classified. Some sorties of SAC's high-altitude UAVs during the war were of particular importance. Early on, in 1965, a Ryan SPA modified to look like a Lockheed U-2 on radar and equipped with many antennas, sensors and telemetry equipment was deliberately sacrificed to an SA-2 missile near Vinh, North Vietnam. The full Russian-made radar information – including acquisition, guidance, even the fusing signal and blast over pressures – was transmitted to an RB-47 flying over the Gulf of Tonkin. This material later provided US air crews with the best radar warning and jamming gear for their survival. The pilot of a 'real' U-2 which was flying well behind the sacrificial Firebee watched the SA-2 streak up and destroy the offered gift. On landing, he said in no certain terms that a UAV should fly all the missions over that particular area!

A new use for high-altitude UAVs arose during 1970 after the loss of an RC-121 communications intelligence (COMMINT) monitoring aircraft above the Yellow Sea. The installation of a COMMINT package in a UAV, which allowed it to listen in to enemy radio messages, also included relay and control equipment, and additional fuel loaded in drop tanks. This provided an eight-hour eavesdropping capability above 60,000 ft, with operations from Osan, South Korea.

For several years prior to Operation Linebacker (the heavy bombing of North Vietnamese targets), the majority of UAV sorties had been of the low-altitude variety, because weather often precluded SR-71 high-altitude or overhead satellite photography. UAVs also were used to deliver leaflets directly over cities, including Hanoi, a mission affectionately known as 'bullshit bombing'. During Linebacker they flew four sorties a day, covering Haiphong and Hanoi targets, with each mission at altitudes below 500 ft.

When Admiral Thomas Moorer, then Chairman of the Joint Chiefs of Staff, briefed Congress on Linebacker's results, he used photos obtained by the UAVs to show that they had not bombed the French Embassy or other sensitive locations, rather they had hit rail sidings, power plants, etc. 'This UAV imagery was the only bomb damage assessment (BDA) available when the chips were down,' he reported.

Perhaps the most telling of John Dale's comments was that 'the biggest supporters of UAVs were fighter/recce types who had been over Hanoi and did not want to go back when a piece of machinery could do the job without drawing blood'.

A North Vietnamese power pylon taken by a Ryan SB-147SB-12 as it flew under the power lines on 12 October 1968. (Teledyne Ryan)

Far left
A Soviet-built SA-2 missile at close quarters.

FIREBEE BOMBERS

A BQM-34B 'Sad Hippo' Pathfinder, fitted with a low-light TV camera in the nose, being loaded with Stubby Hobos during cold-weather trials in May 1974. This unmanned aircraft could have provided the basis for a whole generation of unmanned bombers in the 1980s. They would definitely have been capable of defeating the Soviet SAM threat. However, the technology required was so cutting edge that it did not receive the necessary funding. (Teledyne Ryan)

A BQM-34A with some of the weapons it was capable of carrying, including Maverick and Stubby Hobo missiles, and Mark 81 and 82 iron bombs. A BQM-34B is in the background. (Teledyne Ryan)

A USAF multi-mission Ryan 234, loaded with a Maverick air-to-ground missile, being carried on the inner-wing pylon of a DC-130E Hercules. (Teledyne Ryan)

COMPASS ARROW – 'A SECRET SOMETHING FALLS TO EARTH'

The panic button is pressed. The warning lights on the control panel light up like a Christmas tree. In an underground bunker, the development centre of a secret USAF stealth aircraft, the watching engineers and officers realize that their prototype aircraft is out of control. The decision is taken to remotely deploy the 100-foot emergency recovery parachute. An Air Force C-130 Hercules transport with security and engineering staff is vectored to the point where the aircraft last checked in. On board the Hercules all eyes search the sky for the tell-tale orange and white parachute. Finally, it is spotted but all the C-130 pilot, Major Ken Beckner, can say is, 'I don't like it... I don't like it.' As he banks the aircraft steeply the other members of the crew realize what he means when they see that the parachute and its payload is coming down on top of the Los Alamos Atomic Energy Commission Complex with its plutonium processing plant. The parachuting aircraft is leaking jet fuel and there is a severe danger of a major fire. Luckily a gust of wind comes out of nowhere, the aircraft misses the many H-Bombs' worth of plutonium and it comes gently to rest on a roadway within the wired-off security area.

Although this may sound a little like the beginning of a Clancyesque thriller it is not fiction – this event actually happened. The date was 5 August 1969 and the aircraft in question was a prototype of a new ultra-secret Teledyne Ryan Model 154 unmanned reconnaissance aircraft.

The good news was quickly radioed back to base – no one was hurt – no damage to property. The bad news was that it had landed just yards from the fence and within easy view of a public access road. Not only that but the floating plane and its circling C-130 companion had attracted the attention of the local inhabitants, a large crowd had gathered to see what was going on and snapshots were taken before the surprised Los Alamos security officials could hide the vehicle under a large cover. The C-130 landed at a nearby commerical airfield. The engineers and security people hired a couple of rental cars and rushed off to Los Alamos to retreive their errant aircraft.

The USAF information office went into action but surprisingly it took four hours to release a disinformation statement by which time it was too late to quiet the local newspapers and radio. A damage limitation exercise was not helped when a local Congressman wanted to know if all the FAA regulations concerning flight plans had been met.

National Security considerations prevailed and eventually the Model 154 Compass Arrow quietly withdrew back into its secret world without mention of its all-important stealth characteristics.

Specifically designed to overfly communist China the Ryan Model 154 pushed the state of the art to its limit in order to satisfy the US Air Force requirement to perform a high-altitude, long-range, photographic reconnaissance mission deep inside China. This meant overflying areas covered by enemy fighters and SAMs. The 154 therefore needed to fly at high altitude, 78,000 feet, and was designed for a minimum radar and heat signature, i.e. stealth.

Similar to its Firebee cousin, the Model 154 was launched from under the wing of a DC-130E director aircraft and could be snatched in mid-air by a MARS helicopter or land softly on the ground using air-bags. Officially designated the AQM-91, the 154 had a length of only 34 ft and

Far left
Prototype Ryan Model
154 on its trolley.

Left
The Recovery System was
a very large parachute.

A Model 154 after its
MARS mid-air retrieval.

High altitude and early
stealth technology would
have made this a difficult
target.

Far left
A DC-130 with a heavy load.

Left
The small tail parachute helped to stabilise the 154 as the helicopter brought it home.

Bottom
Designed for the dangerous overflights of communist China, the Model 154 was never allowed to show if it had 'the right stuff'.

wingspan of 47 ft with which it achieved an amazing range of 2,000 nautical miles plus another hundred miles during the unpowered glide phase. The KA-80A camera system could take a stream of pictures with a swath of 43 miles over a 1,720-mile stretch of rice paddies and A-bomb test sites and had an optical resolution of one foot directly under the flight path.

Dropped from the DC-130 at an altitude of 15–25,000 ft while still 200–300 miles from the Communist border the 154 had the most sophisticated internal navigation system, Guidance Navigation System (GNS), that the US electronics industry could design. It had brand new digital technology and was a quantum leap forward in terms of accuracy compared to its contemporary Vietnam Firebees. On returning to a predetermined recovery area the DC-130 could take control of the aircraft via an encoded microwave link and an on-board pilot would fly it towards the waiting pickup helicopter.

Top secret tests conducted at locations such as Holloman AFB revealed that enemy-designed radar found the 154 almost impossible to get a lock on.

Using their experience with the Firebees over Vietnam, Ryan engineers minimized the radar cross-section of the 154 airframe 'by contouring the structural shapes, shadowing the engine intake and exhaust ducts and by using radiation-transparent and radiation-absorption materials. Infrared suppression has been achieved by positioning the engine on the top area of the aircraft, extending the fuselage aft of the engine, shadowing the tailpipe by the twin-canted vertical fins and using engine inlet air to cool the engine ejector nozzle.'

Because it was a purpose-built reconnaissance vehichle with highly secret and sophisticated systems and not a conversion of an expendable target aircraft, the Compass Arrow was also designed to have a self-destruct system.

After initial testing it was decided to find out if the system was 'ready to deploy'. This job was given to the USAF 100th Strategic Reconnaissance Wing which received the nickname 'Busy Robot' for the duration and was accomplished between August and December 1971. 'The eight-mission test schedule was staged out of Davis-Monthan Air Force Base with launch and recovery accomplished at Edwards Flight Test Centre. Range co-ordination and MARS helicopter support were provided by the 6514th Test Squadron.' The test missions were flown over California and Arizona and lasted 3.5 to 4 hours. The distance covered was typically 1,600 to 1,800 nautical miles and altitudes up to 81,000 feet were reached. The final report stated:

Operationally, the AQM-91A is capable of performing high altitude photo reconnaissance missions of 4 hours flight duration, 3.1 hours camera duration, and 1900 nautical miles in length. The Guidance Navigation System (GNS) is capable of executing all programmed functions and directing the Special Purpose Aircraft (SPA) over the planned track with a high degree of accuracy. In addition, because of outstanding vehicle stability, higher photo resolution and improved photo overlap consistency is achieved. Together the AQM-91A and KA-80A scorer provide an excellent unmanned strategic reconnaissance system.

GNS performance was excellent and in the

primary Doppler/Inertial mode navigational accuracy of less than one-half of one per cent of distance travelled can be expected.

Further tests were carried out at the Electronic Warfare Tactical Environment Simulation (EWTES), Naval Weapons Center, China Lake, California, and confirmed a high performance against a variety of simulated Soviet SAM systems including Fansong B and E radar and associated equipment of SA-2 Guideline missiles.

The Compass Arrow was now ready to deploy.

However, with the conflict in South East Asia quickly drawing to a close, President Nixon, aided by his Secretary of State, Kissinger, wanted a closer relationship with communist China. The result of this executive decision went further than high profile 'ping pong diplomacy', it put the 154's mission on hold.

Keen to prove the worth of its latest and best product, Ryan and its supporters in the military tried getting it tasked with missions over Cuba or even the Middle East. Instead it was relegated to ready-alert basis at Davis-Monthan AFB, nick-named the 'Bone Yard' because that is where old aeroplanes go to die. Some time later Compass Arrow was 'disappeared' from the aviation scene leaving nothing behind it but the promise of great things.

Politics prevented the use of the Compass Arrow and even its very existence was a source of embarrassment in an era of rapprochement with the communist Chinese. Added to which the technology embodied within this craft was much too secret to allow it to surface into the public domain. Therefore its fate, which is still unconfirmed, according to knowledgable sources

was that the USAF sent what remained of the 28 Model 154s to be guillotined and melted down at an Air Force facility near Tucson, Arizona. It is rumoured that only the engines were salvaged.

This project is a classic tale of the secret world of unmanned air vehicles.

Later in this book it will be claimed that the USA currently have secret UAV projects hidden away from prying eyes and what the Compass Arrow points to is that it is still possible that 'something secret' may fall to earth at any time.

Engineers check the systems on the 154 prior to the test flight.

The beleaguered Israelis were quick to appreciate the value of UAVs. Following the Six-Day War in June 1967 and the War of Attrition on the Suez Canal in 1969/70, a team of Israeli Air Force officers was briefed on the success of surveillance UAVs over South-East Asia and secretly invited to observe Firebee tests in New Mexico.

Impressed by what they saw, and under great security, the Israeli Air Force signed a contract in

Pion

1970 to purchase 12 modified Firebees, designated 1241s. The first flight trials in Israel were carried out at a secret location in the Sinai desert a year later. By September 1971 the Israeli Air Force was operating missions over surface-to-air missile sites in Egypt. The UAVs played an important role in the October 1973 Yom Kippur War both as reconnaissance vehicles and, in some desperate cases, as decoys.

It was reported that the Israelis used Firebees

armed with Shrike anti-radar missiles to lead attacks against Egyptian air defences and that one Firebee was targeted by 32 surface-to-air missiles before it returned safely to its base. Roaming from Cairo to Damascus, the Firebees came back with valuable information.

A second batch of 1241s was delivered to Israel in the 1980s. It is reported that a quantity of surplus USAF and US Navy Firebee 1471s and TFs were also acquired, but apparently none was

deployed in Israel. While the Firebee 1241s are still on the Israeli Air Force's inventory, the emphasis has moved to the development of a family of indigenous UAVs. Having taken full note of the sub-scale, low-cost UAVs that were evaluated by the US Navy in the late 1950s, Israel purchased several US Prairie mini-UAVs which could carry TV and laser target designators and forward-looking infrared (FLIR) imaging equipment. By utilizing available off-the-shelf components, such as Austrian lightweight piston engines, American radio-control units and Japanese TV cameras, Israeli designers were soon launching prototype UAVs from improvised ramps.

In 1978 Israel Aircraft Industries (IAI) built its first practical, cost-effective, short-range, tactical UAV, the Mastiff. With a 13 ft 9 in wing-span, this twin-boomed, piston-engined aircraft was built largely of glass fibre to give it an extremely low radar signature. The Mastiff was followed by the slightly larger Scout. It was capable of transmitting real-time data. It also had a TV camera or FLIR in a central turret, providing 360° degree surveillance. The Scout was the Israeli armed forces' principal

Syrian-supported PLO from Lebanon by mid-1982.

On 9 June 1982 the Israeli Air Force launched a series of attacks against the Syrian SA-6 sites in the Beka'a Valley. The exact position of these had been detected by the Scout UAVs, which had enticed the Syrians to

eer

UAVs

>>>

tactical UAV from 1976 to 1996, when it in turn was replaced by the longer-endurance, day-and-night capable Searcher.

In May 1981 Israel sent Firebees over Syrian SA-6 missile batteries which had been deployed in Lebanon's Beka'a Valley. One was shot down by a high-speed SA-6. By the year end, Israel admitted to losing three UAVs. At the same time, Scouts working with IDF/AF RF-4E Phantoms continued to probe Syrian air defences, recording data for future reference.

Following a year of mounting tension between the two countries, Israel felt confident enough to mount Operation Peace for Galilee to drive the

switch on their radar and communications systems. The Scouts relayed this information to airborne E-2C Hawkeyes. In the resulting air attacks by F-4s, A-4s and Kfirs, no Israeli pilot was shot down and no UAV was lost. The raids were in support of Israel's invasion of southern Lebanon, during the planning of which UAVs played a key role. Their small size and low radar signature made them almost impossible to shoot down. Also, their electronic microwave link proved to be unjammable by the Syrians. During the seven-week operation, Israel destroyed 17 of

Syria's 19 SA-6 sites, and shot down a total of 85 Syrian fighters for the loss of three of their own. Several UAVs were lost during the campaign, but all of them were attributed to technical problems.

Despite the overwhelming defeat of Syrian forces in 1982, more than ten years of conflict followed against Hizbollah terrorists operating from southern Lebanon, culminating in Operation Grapes of Wrath in April 1996. Searcher UAVs carried out a 24-hour watch out during the 16-day artillery war between Israeli and Hizbollah gunners across the security zone of southern Lebanon. Some of the UAVs were controlled from IAI Arava early-warning 'mother' aircraft. The

Above left
The Swiss Ranger UAV system's mobile receiving unit (MRU) which relays the real-time data to the GCS and army headquarters. (Oerlikon)

Above middle
The spacious hi-tech interior of the Ranger UAV system's mobile GCS. Compare it with the more austere Hunter and Pioneer GCSs. (Oerlikon)

Above right
Another vital component of a modern UAV system is the remote communications terminal (RCT). This one belongs to the Swiss Ranger system. (Oerlikon)

Right
The Oerlikon Ranger tactical UAV ready for take-off from its hydraulic catapult which is mounted on a standard Swiss Army truck. (Oerlikon)

dramatic visual images relayed by the Israeli UAVs during Operation Grapes of Wrath became a familiar sight to TV viewers around the world. Israeli UAVs had flown more than 1,200 hours in bad weather with no losses and largely dictated the nature of the battle.

DESERT STORM AND THE PIONEER FAMILY

The Israeli UAVs spawned a whole family of twin-boomed look-alikes, the most successful of which was the Pioneer. In the late 1980s, the US Navy had identified a requirement for an inexpensive, unmanned targeting vehicle with a reconnaissance capability, so it ordered the IAI-designed Pioneer short-range, tactical UAV. At least, this is the official version of the story; the unofficial one is much more interesting. During two air strikes against 'terrorist' positions in the Beka'a Valley the

US Navy had lost three of its planes. The admiral on the US aircraft carrier was not amused and asked for a briefing from Israeli intelligence about how they operated over the area with seeming immunity. A few days later the Israeli officers arrived and they began their presentation by playing a videotape which contained highlights of events on the carrier over the previous days. Among these clips were apparently close-ups of the admiral himself on the bridge. Unbeknown to the carrier task force, a little UAV had been shadowing them since they had requested the intelligence briefing. Having seen enough, the admiral stood up and said, 'We've got to have whatever this is!'

Therefore, Pioneers were on hand for Operation Desert Storm. They operated from US Navy battleships and US Marine assault ships, and with the US Army in the desert. Day and night,

US Navy Pioneers launching from a warship using rocket-assisted take-off (RATO). Pioneers from the three US services flew more than 300 Desert Storm combat missions. (Israeli Aircraft Industries)

VMU-2 Pioneers lined up at an airstrip at Marine Camp Lejeune in South Carolina. (David Oliver)

Pioneer tactical UAVs belonging to the US Marine Corps VMU-2 Squadron based in Virginia. (David Oliver)

A Pioneer of VMU-1 in Bosnia. It has its engine running and is ready to be launched from its mobile catapult ramp. (David Oliver)

A US Navy Pioneer prior to launching from the forward deck of the battleship USS Missouri during an attack on Iraqi positions in Kuwait. The Pioneers were used for spotting naval gunfire and battlefield-damage assessment (BDA). (AAI)

they provided highly valued real-time reconnaissance, surveillance and target acquisition, as well as battle-damage assessment (BDA). They observed the Iraqi incursion into Saudi Arabia at Kaffjia and helped to direct the artillery and helicopters that persuaded the invaders to leave town.

The Pioneers often worked with the USAF's Joint Surveillance Target Attack Radar Systems (J-STARS) to confirm high-priority mobile targets detected by the E-8s' synthetic aperture radar (SAR).

The Pioneers took off from makeshift runways and carrier flight decks; they were rocket-boosted from warships or catapulted from ramps in the desert. They flew a total of 533 operational sorties during the Gulf War, but not without loss. Twelve were destroyed and a further 14 damaged – but at no human cost. The US Marine Corps subsequently deployed their UAVs during UN operations over Haiti and Bosnia.

The latest IAI-inspired developments include the Swiss government's Ranger; the TRW Inc./IAI twin-engined Hunter, designed to replace the US Navy and Marine Corps' Pioneers; AAI's Shadow ordered by Turkey and Romania; the Hungarian/Czech Sojka III, and Israel's own long-range, high-altitude Heron which completed a record-breaking 51-hour 21-minute flight in May

US Army and Marine Corps technicians demonstrate the operation of the mobile ground-control station (GCS) of the Hunter UAV system. (TRW)

1995. The Indian government also designed its own twin-boomer, the Nishant, but as a precaution it has also ordered the IAI Searcher for the Indian Army and may produce the type under licence in the future.

The government of India's troubled southern neighbour, Sri Lanka, has been fighting the Tamil Tigers for the last 13 years with the aid of Searcher UAVs, five of which are operated by the Sri Lankan Air Force.

Even Teledyne Ryan built an 'affordable', twin-boomed, single-piston pusher-engined UAV, the Model 410. This first flew in 1988 with a pilot on board, before making its first unmanned flight in 1992. The private-venture 410 has not yet been put into production. Nearly all these UAVs, powered by 25–100 hp piston engines, have fixed, wheeled undercarriages. They can take off from short runways, be catapulted from a ramp, or be rocket-assisted from a rail which is usually mounted on a standard army truck. They are able to land on runways using a hook and arrester wire, or be retrieved by a net on ships. Some can be recovered by parachute in an emergency.

South Africa has also developed a successful UAV with Israeli assistance. Having evaluated the IAI Scout in the early 1980s, the South African Defence Force came up with a requirement for a long-range, mobile, self-contained system that

The twin-engined Hunter has been designed as a joint tactical (JT) UAV to replace US Army and Marine Corps Pioneers. Here one is taking off for a systems-proving flight in Arizona. (TRW)

The powerful, composite-constructed Kentron Seeker, South Africa's capable long-range, tactical UAV, was battle-proven in Angola. Here is one with its payload dome extended. (Denel)

A US Army Pioneer, used for target location, being launched from its ramp at a forward operating base (FOB) in the desert during the Gulf War. (Israeli Aircraft Industries)

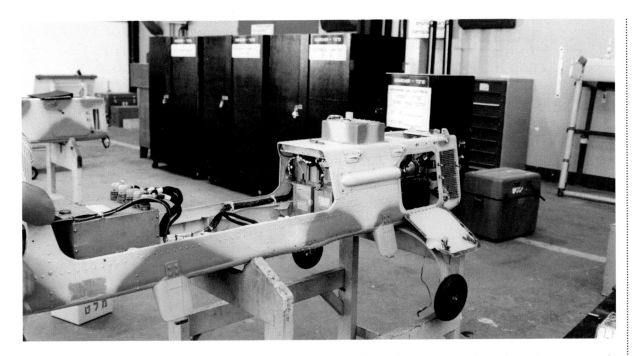

The main fuselage of a Searcher on the Malat production line at Ben Gurion Airport, showing the large payload bay forward of the pusher engine. (Simon Watson)

would benefit from its indigenous arms technology – the Kentron Seeker. Seekers were used operationally in Angola by the South African Air Force's 10 Squadron, which had been reformed at Potchefstroom in 1986. It flew 20 long-range combat missions over Angola between September and October 1987 with the loss of three UAVs. By the end of the Angolan conflict a year later, many lessons had been learned and the Seeker was extensively modified with a more powerful engine, better payload – which included a gyrostatically controlled thermal-imaging system (TIS) – and increased infrared (IR) protection. The result is a rugged all-weather UAV which costs considerably less to operate than the IAI Searcher.

In 1994 South African Defence Force Seekers were used to monitor the first multiracial elections, operating over cities such as Johannesburg and Pretoria. During the 17-day deployment, the former 10 Squadron Seekers, fitted with transponders for civilian-controlled airspace, flew 14 day-and-night missions, the longest of which was 4 hours 14 minutes.

The policing operations have been recently extended to cover gang warfare that has broken out in disputed areas of KwaZulu-Natal. Operation Jambo is a combined army, air force and police operation. The security forces spend four to six weeks in the field with a typical Seeker unit comprising three UAVs, a mobile control centre and a crew of nine. The Seeker's efficient TIS can send clear pictures from 18,000 ft, day or night. It can operate up to 120 miles from the control centre, loiter in the target area for 6 hours and has an automatic 'return-home' system activated in the event of a communications breakdown.

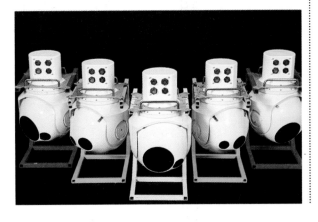

A selection of thermal-imaging, IR- and TV-sensor payloads that can be carried by the Kentron Seeker UAV. (Denel)

DESERT STORM

In response to the Iraqi invasion of Kuwait in August 1990, the largest UN-backed force seen since the Korean War was assembled in the Gulf. The US deployed its most advanced surveillance assets including joint service Pioneer UAVs. Operated from mobile launchers in the desert, the decks of USN battleships and Marine assault carriers, Pioneer was, according to Marine Corps commander Lt Gen. Boomer, 'the single most important intelligence collector' during operations *Desert Shield* and *Storm*. Iraqi soldiers actually surrendered to a Pioneer during the battle for Kuwait. Twelve were lost in the Gulf War. The US army also used the Pointer micro-UAV, but bad weather and high winds made it less effective. More successful were the Northrop BQM-74C target drones used by the USAF's 4468th Tactical Reconnaissance Group as decoys in the opening hours of Operation *Desert Storm*.

France used its simple but effective MART Mk 1 which stood up to the rigours of desert operations well, while the British Army had to rely on the twenty-year-old Canadair CL-89 system, nicknamed the 'Midge'.

The Gulf War proved to be an important watershed in UAV operations and directly led to the development of Predator, DarkStar and Global Hawk.

Main picture
Northrop decoys in the desert.

Insert top
Pioneer was deemed one of the great success stories of operation Desert Storm even turning the 16-inch guns of the US Navy WW2 battleships into effective and accurate weapons.

Insert bottom
The US Army, Navy and Marine Corps made exten-sive use of IAI Pioneer UAVs. This one is being prepared for launching from its mobile hydraulic ramp during Operation Desert Storm. (Israeli Aircraft Industries)

Using many of the E-Hunter's components, an IAI Heron multi-purpose, all-weather, long-endurance UAV completed a test flight of more than 51 hours in 1995. (Israeli Aircraft Industries)

Another South African company, ATE, has developed a small battlefield observation UAV for artillery targeting, known as the Vulture. Powered by a 22 hp piston engine, it can be deployed in 30 minutes by a four-man crew and launched from a unique atmospheric launcher.

RUSSIA

The Soviet Union was slow to recognize the importance of UAVs. Although some might suggest that this came from a philosophy which did not shirk from placing people in dangerous situations, it was more likely to have been the lack of Russian computer prowess that was to blame. The Soviet Union, as it was at the time, did produce a tactical, single-use reconnaissance UAV powered by a 6,000 lb thrust RD-9 turbojet in the late 1950s, the Lavochkin La-17R. It was launched

from a ramp developed from the undercarriage of a World War Two 85 mm anti-aircraft gun, and it landed on its engine nacelle, which was hung under the fuselage. Despite its short range and limited capability and the expense of only being used once, the La-17R was operated by the Soviet Army for nearly 20 years.

In 1958 Aleksei Tupolev, son of the Tupolev Design Bureau's founder, set up a 'pilotless aircraft division' to design missiles for strike,

reconnaissance and space activities.

The first successful tactical reconnaissance missile, developed after a series of failures in the 1960s, was the Tu-143. With similar dimensions to those of the Firebee, the Tu-143 *Reis* (voyage) first flew in 1972. It was powered by a 1,279 lb thrust TR3-117 turbojet and carried a payload comprising an optical camera and a TV camera or radiation monitor. Launched from a mobile platform with a single launch rocket, the Tu-143 cruised at 550 mph at an altitude of 300 to 10,000 ft, but it only had a maximum range of 120 miles or a duration of 13 minutes! It was recovered by parachute.

Despite its limited performance, nearly 1,000 Tu-143s were produced between 1973 and 1989. Most were used as target drones, and exported to

Top and bottom
The short-range Tu-143 Reis (Voyage) was a small version of the Tu-141, with an endurance of only 13 minutes! It took off from a mobile launcher using RATO, and it was recovered by parachute. (RART)

Left
One of the first reconnaissance UAVs used by the USSR's Army was the single-use Lavochkin La-17R, which was launched from a converted World War Two AAA gun platform. (Yefim Gordon/RART)

The Yak-60 Schmel (Bumblebee) was a more powerful Bee with sprung undercarriage legs instead of the Yak-60S's skids. It was ordered by the Russian Army. (RART)

Czechoslovakia, Romania and Syria. The Tu-143 was succeeded by the Tu-141 *Strizh* (swift), a longer-range development of the *Reis* with folding wings. Powered by a 4,409 lb thrust R-17A turbojet which gave it a cruising speed of 650 mph at altitudes between 200 and 20,000 ft, the Tu-141 had a range of 620 miles. Its payload comprised two TV cameras, side-looking radar (SLAR) and an infrared line scanner (IRLS) or a radiation monitor. First flown in 1975, some 150 were built before production ceased at the Kharkov factory N135 in 1989. It remains in limited service in Russia and the Ukraine.

The Tu-243 and Tu-300 *Korshun* (kite) are further derivatives of the *Reis* with improved endurance and sensor payloads intended to replace the *Strizh* UAV system.

Having watched its ally, Syria, being humiliated in southern Lebanon in 1982 by Israeli 'model aircraft' spotting SAMs for its air force to destroy, the Soviet Union issued the Yakovlev Design Bureau with a directive to construct a short-range tactical UAV in the Scout class 'within a year'.

Yakovlev's only previous experience of unmanned aircraft was the production of a pilotless version of its ultra-high-altitude reconnaissance Yak-25RV designed to rival the American U-2 in the late 1950s. A remotely piloted version of the Flashlight-C flown in the mid-1960s, the RV-11, it carried a control to feed autopilot commands from a 'pilot' flying in a modified Yak-30 two-seater which was the unsuccessful competitor for the contract to be adopted as the Soviet Air Force's standard jet trainer, won by the Czechoslovak L-29.

The tactical UAV programme, led by another son of a famous designer, Sergei Yakovlev,

stipulated that the UAV's launch weight would be limited to 220 lb. This meant that a high proportion of the aircraft would have to be made of new, unproven composite materials. After five years of development, a pre-production UAV, the DPLA-60S *Pchela* (bee) was issued to units of the Soviet Army and Air Force, with favourable results. In 1984 work began on a slightly larger version, known as the *Shmel* (bumblebee). Powered by a 32 hp Samara P-032 piston engine, the Yakovlev UAV resembled a torpedo with a shrouded two-blade propeller, an 11-foot shoulder-mounted wing, and standing on four sprung legs. The reconnaissance payload fitted in the nose of the torpedo consisted of a day-and-night TV camera mounted in a turret, giving a 3° to 30° field of view, an IRLS and an early-warning jammer. The *Shmel* was designed to be deployed in a container on the top of a tracked armoured vehicle which also accommodates the launch rail and the control station. It is recovered by parachute. After initial launch failures during its rocket-boosted launch from the vehicle-mounted rail, government evaluations were finally completed in 1989 and series production commenced the following year. Its entry into front-line service with the Russian Army coincided with the swingeing cutbacks imposed on the armed forces, and deliveries have been slow. However,

an instrumented target-acquisition version entered limited production in 1994 and the *Shmel* is reported to have been ordered by Syria.

Several variations of the *Shmel* have been designed by the Yakovlev bureau, including a twin-boom version with wheeled undercarriage able to take off and land on a runway, and a rotary-wing variant named the *Zhavoronok* (skylark), neither of which has progressed beyond the mock-up stage.

The bureau recently revealed several innovative UAV designs whose progress beyond the drawing board has been restricted by lack of funds. The first, named *Kolobri* (hummingbird) was designed as a stealthy long-range replacement for the *Shmel* featuring a low-mounted 20-foot span swept wing, a flat pointed fuselage, T-tail and retractable tricycle undercarriage. It would be powered by a 75 hp Voronezh M-29 pusher piston engine, have spacious sensor bays and an endurance of eight hours. With the lack of military backing the *Kolobri*

is being offered to the civil market for atmospheric and environmental monitoring. An even more advanced Yakovlev UAV project is the *Albatros*, a high-speed, tilt-rotor with an inverted V-tail.

A more conventional rotary-wing UAV is being developed by the innovative Russian helicopter designer Kamov as a joint-venture project with Daewoo of South Korea. Kamov is flight-testing the coaxial, rotary-wing UAV powered by a 60 hp piston engine which is designed for similar roles to Bell's Eagle Eye. These capabilities include aerial photography,

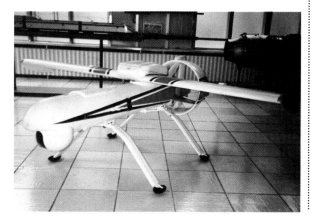

Built in the 1970s, the powerful Tu-123 could cruise at twice the speed of sound at 60,000 ft for 2,000 miles. The nose compartment, carrying the cameras, was parachuted to the ground. (RART)

Top right
The rear of the Yak-60S, showing the ducted propeller driven by a 20 hp Samara P-020 piston engine. (RART)

BEHIND THE IRON AND BAMBOO CURTAINS

With the end of the Cold War we now know that the Soviet Union lagged a long way behind the USA, and in particular Israel in the development and deployment of practical UAVs. Most were large, unsophisticated jet or rocket-powered vehicles with very limited range and sensor payloads.

Ironically, it was not until the end of the Soviet Union was in sight that its first practical short-range tactical UAV was developed by the Yakovlev Design Bureau.

Red China has, if anything, been even slower at recognizing the value of surveillance UAVs although a Searcher look-alike was shown at the 1996 Zhuhai Air Show.

The most successful tactical UAV currently produced by former WarPac countries is the twin-boom Omnipol Sojka III jointly developed by Hungary and Czechoslovakia.

Right
The Tu-141 Strizh (Swift) was a long-range, multi-purpose UAV developed by the Tupolev Design Bureau in the 1970s. It remains in limited service in Russia and the Ukraine. (Mort Stanley/RART)

Far right
This Chinese-built Firebee look-alike is carried under the wing of a PLAF Tu-4 bomber, itself a Soviet copy of the American B-29 Superfortress.

Left
A model of Yakovlev's stealthy, long-range Kolibri (Hummingbird), which resembles a scaled-down IAI Heron.

Insert
This Soviet La-17R reconnaissance UAV was also built in China under licence. Known as the KJ-1, it is still in prod-uction for the PLA. (R Walg)

Bottom left
The Omnipol Sojka III, originally a joint venture between Czechoslovakia and Hungary, is now in production for the Czech Army. (Omnipol)

communications relay, crop spraying, search and rescue, and aerial supply. A smaller version, the Ka-137, has also been built.

Russia's Kazan Research Centre has designed a small UAV, the R90. Weighing only 100 lb, it is powered by a 12 lb thrust pulse-jet. It also has cruise missile-type folding wings and tail surfaces which deploy when it is launched from a cylinder carried under the wing of a carrier aircraft. This mini stand-off reconnaissance UAV has a mission radius of only ten miles, after which it is recovered by parachute.

CHINA

Communist China got into the UAV business thanks to the Vietnam War and the deployment during that conflict of the most successful operational UAV in history, Teledyne Ryan's Firebee.

Unmanned 'spy plane' missions over North Vietnam and China began in August 1962 under the code-name Lightning Bugs. On 15 November 1964, Firebee 147B-19 was shot down by Chinese

MiGs as it climbed to its programmed altitude over central south China. The announcement was greeted with disbelief by the US press because it was not aware that any unmanned aircraft was capable of such long-range flights.

On 2 January 1965 a second 147B was shot down in similar circumstances, and a third on 31 March. The second Firebee was put on public display in Beijing three months later, and the following day yet another was lost, with a fifth falling to Chinese fighters on 18 April. Three of the American UAVs were displayed together in Beijing. Before the year was out a sixth 147B was shot down over Hainan Island by Chinese Navy fighters. Although the Lightning Bugs remained a classified programme in the USA, some 25 Firebees, including the high-altitude 147H, were brought down over China before the fall of Saigon in April 1975. China was impressed by the success of the Firebees, which had flown some 3,500 missions over China and North Vietnam in 11 years of conflict. By a process of reverse engineering using the shot-down Firebees, it produced an almost identical copy. Chinese Tu-4 bombers, which were in turn Russian copies of the American Boeing B-29, were used to air-launch the Firebee look-alikes, a supersonic version of which was built in the 1980s.

China has been building the Soviet Lavoshkin La-17R single-use reconnaissance UAV under licence since the 1960s, and it has continued to develop this jet-powered aircraft. The latest version, the CK-1C, remains in production for the People's Liberation Army.

In the late 1980s, China's first indigenous UAV, designed by the Xian ASN Technical Group, took to the air. The D-4, a small monoplane UAV powered by a 30 hp piston-engine, is for civilian aerial surveying. It was later developed into the surveillance UAV ASN-105 for

the army. The group recently revealed the ASN-206 day/night battlefield surveillance and targeting UAV, which shows more than a passing resemblance to South Africa's Seeker. The twin-boom ASN-206 is powered by a 50 hp HS-700 pusher engine. It has an 18-foot wing-span, an endurance of 8 hours and a maximum range of 95 miles, depending on the payload. According to its chief designer, Zhang Yu Zhou, the ASN-206 is only available for export, although it would be surprising if it did not end up on the army's inventory in the near future.

WESTERN EUROPE

France took the lead in European UAV development in the 1960s with the Nord R-20, a battlefield reconnaissance development of the Nord GT-20, a Firebee look-alike, target/UAV. Both the R-20 and GT-20 were powered by an 880 lb thrust

A longer-range variant of the Crecerelle, the Sperwer seen being catapult-launched. It is being developed for the Dutch Army. (Sagem)

The Italian Meteor company has a long history of producing UAVs, the latest being the Mirach 26 short-range twin-boomer. (Meteor)

Turbomeca Marbore turbojet. Launched from a short ramp fitted on a standard French Army lorry, it carried standard NATO recce cameras over a distance of 100 miles, flying at 3,000 ft. Aerospatiale, which later absorbed Nord Aviation, now produces a range of small, short-range, tactical UAVs, such as the Flibuste.

The simple but effective Altec MART (Mini Avion de Reconnaissance Telepilote) short-range, battlefield-reconnaissance and target-acquisition UAV first entered service with the French 8th Artillery Regiment in 1990. The MART Mark I formed part of France's Draguet Division during the 1991 Gulf War. The MART Mark II, incorporating upgrades as a result of lessons learned from Desert Storm operations, is operated by the 6th Artillery Regiment.

Another French UAV to gain recent operational experience in a combat environment was the CAC Fox AT-1. In May 1993 the United Nations Protection Force (UNPROFOR) issued a requirement for a lightweight, short-range UAV for operations over Bosnia. The Fox AT-1 was selected and operated by the 3rd French Battalion at Bihac for six months. Four Fox AT-Is, equipped with colour TV cameras and GPS receivers, flew most of their daylight missions, which averaged 45 minutes, at below 1,500 ft. One was shot down some ten miles from its launch site.

Again lessons learned from combat experience have been incorporated into the Fox AT-2 , and an electronic-warfare variant has also been developed. More than 650 Fox UAVs have been ordered to date. The same company has developed the Heliot, an unmanned system utilizing the Italian Dragon Fly, a low-cost, two-seat helicopter powered by a 105 hp Hirth piston engine. For missions where the risk to a pilot is considered unacceptable, a remote-control unit and four-axis stabilization avionics allow the pilot to be replaced with an increased payload capacity. The Dragon Fly becomes a surveillance or electronic-warfare UAV able to fly day or night up to 30 miles from its take-off point. In its unmanned version, the Heliot system comprises a mobile ground station which is capable of towing a trailer carrying two helicopters. The whole system is air-transportable, highly mobile and suitable for ground- or ship-based missions.

The French Sagem company is building the Crecerelle, a divisional level surveillance UAV which has a transmission range of 45 miles and an endurance of up to five hours. This delta-wing UAV, powered by a 26 hp piston engine, was developed from the UK's successful Banshee target drone and it is in service with the French Army. Sagem is also developing the Sperwer, a medium-range, battlefield-surveillance and target-acquisition UAV system with a six-hour endurance, for the Dutch armed forces, as well as the Alvis rotary-engined Marula, a radar jammer and potentially Europe's first attack UAV, which can carry a pre-fragmented warhead. In co-operation with General Dynamics, Sagem is to produce a European variant of the Predator endurance-mission UAV (see Chapter 14) under the name Horus.

Techno Sud Industries, part of France's Thomson-CFS aerospace giant, is developing a small rotary-wing UAV powered by a two-stroke engine, the Vigilant 2000, which can carry an 18 lb payload, aimed at both the military and the civil markets.

France is also a 40 per cent partner, along with Germany, in the Brevel, a small, stealthy,

short-range UAV with an endurance of ten hours. Powered by a 29 hp Sachs piston engine, the Brevel, which is rocket-boost launched from a truck-mounted container and recovered by parachute, will have a sophisticated sensor package. It is scheduled to enter service with the French and German armies by 1998.

A simpler export version of the Brevel, the Tucan-95, is being developed by the Franco-German company STN Atlas.

The Dornier company first designed a rotary-wing UAV, the Do-32U based on the innovative Gyrodyne QH-50D (see page 27), in the 1970s and it continued the theme with the Kiebitz and Geamos in the 1980s. The latest in the line, the Seamos, is a product of the Dornier division of Dasa, and it is designed to meet the NATO naval vertical take-off and recovery (VTOR) UAV system. This requirement is programmed to enter service within the next ten years for operation on new generation frigates from Germany, France, Britain, Italy, the Netherlands and Spain. Seamos is a maritime-surveillance, over-the-horizon (OTH), target-acquisition/designation system. Powered by a 420 shp turboshaft driving coaxial rotors, Seamos can carry a weighty 310 lb payload at a maximum speed of 105 mph, and all this with a four-hour endurance.

Another European company with a long history of UAV development, dating back to the early 1960s, is the Italian Meteor CAE company. Starting with a range of small target drones, Meteor built its first reconnaissance drone, the P.1/R, in 1965. Powered by a 110 hp Alfa piston engine and launched by rocket booster from a zero-length ramp, the P.1/R carried its pre-programmed guidance system and cameras in separate underwing pods, the latter being capable of recovery by its own parachute.

Meteor's latest UAVs include the short-range, tactical Mirach 26, another twin-boom design powered by the 27 hp Sachs piston engine driving a pusher prop, and the 330 lb thrust Microturbo turbojet-powered Mirach 150. The latter is a high-speed, 450 mph, medium-range, reconnaissance and target-acquisition UAV with a one-hour endurance. Both types are recovered by parachute and are under evaluation with the Italian Army.

BRITAIN

Despite producing a large number of highly successful target drones, many of them pilotless

A real-time image transmitted from the Brevel seen on a screeen in its system's GCS. (STN)

GEC-Marconi have spent ten years, and many millions of pounds, developing the Phoenix battlefield-surveillance UAV system which has yet to go into service with the British Army. (GEC-Marconi)

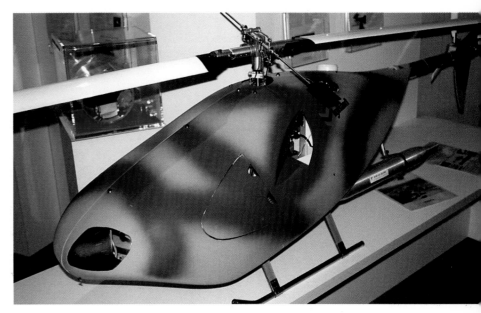

Artist's impression
of an RAF UCAV.

versions of manned aircraft, since the successful Queen Bee (see Chapter 1) which included the Firefly U-8, Meteor U-15/16 and Sea Vixen D-3, Britain has singularly failed to produce and deploy a home-made UAV. Its armed forces bought and operated the highly successful Australian jet-powered Jindivik target drone, which has been in production for nearly five decades, and a series of US-manufactured piston-engined drones, such as the Radioplane KD2R-5 and Northrop Shelduck, for many years before Meggitt Target Technology UK produced the successful Banshee target drone. Meggitt produced the ASR-4 Spectre UAV derived from the compact, delta-wing Banshee, which the French selected as the basis for the Sagem Crecerelle tactical-reconnaissance and target-acquisition UAV. The company has also developed a smaller, low-cost version, the autonomous Phantom, designed for close-range battlefield-surveillance missions.

Over the past decade, Flight Refuelling Ltd, the company which converted ex-RAF and Royal Navy fighters into drones in the 1950s, has built a number of experimental UAVs, including an advanced jet-powered high-speed drone, the ASAT. It has also been developing the Raven, a low-cost surveillance UAV based on the XRAE-1 designed by the former Royal Aircraft Establishment (RAE) at Farnborough.

The same company embarked on the development of a battlefield-targeting UAV for the British Army, known as the Phoenix. Unbelievably, £230 million and more than a decade later, Phoenix, now managed by GEC-Marconi, is still not in

A line-up of brightly coloured RAF unmanned Meteor and U-15 and U-16 target drones at RAF Llanbedr in Wales. (Arthur Pearcy)

operational service. Originally ordered by the Ministry of Defence for the British Army to provide target-acquisition support for the army's AS90 self-propelled 155 mm howitzer and multiple-rocket system (MLRS), Phoenix is an 18-foot span, twin-boomed UAV powered by a 25 hp piston engine, capable of carrying a 110 lb payload, which includes a turret-mounted infrared sensor in a pod beneath the fuselage. Designed to be launched from a truck-mounted pneumatic/hydraulic catapult, recovery is made by parachute. This has proved to be one of Phoenix's many shortcomings. As the payload is carried under the UAV, which has no undercarriage legs or struts to protect it on landing, when the parachute deploys, it was designed to flip the Phoenix on to its back and the landing cushioned by an impact-absorbing dorsal fairing. In trials, unacceptable damage was caused by heavy landings and the resulting collapse of the fairing. To counteract this situation, additional automobile-type deployable air-bags have had to be fitted. These have added to the craft's all-up weight. Other problems have arisen with the data-link interface, and there are now serious doubts about its long-term performance potential. The system was designed before the lessons from Operation Desert Storm were absorbed. In addition, Phoenix has problems with operating in hot and high conditions, and its sensor payload cannot be increased to include a laser designator without a more powerful engine. It is the classic case of too little too late, and Phoenix may yet not rise by its schedule delivery date of 1998.

In December 1996 the British Minister of Defence announced plans for a Future Offensive Air System (FOAS) to replace the RAF Tornado strike fighter force from 2015. One of the options under consideration is an unmanned tactical aircraft (UTA) which would have a primary air-to-ground weapons delivery mission with the flexibility to perform suppression of enemy air defences (SEAD), battle-damage assessment (BDA) and air-interdiction (AI) missions. The UTA would be flown by virtual-reality cockpits installed either on the ground or in advanced concepts of the 'mother' aircraft, such as the E-3 Sentry.

However, for some time there have been rumours that British Aerospace has been working on a number of 'black programmes' for the UK's Defence Evaluation Research Agency (DERA). One of these is a low-cost, high-altitude, long-endurance UAV propelled by solar radiation or ground-beamed radiation.

The project is being developed at BAe's Special Projects Site at Warton, near Preston. Several sightings have been reported over the past 18 months of a triangular UAV, approximately 30 ft in length, flying at height in formation with BAe Tornado fighters over Britain's west coasts. It has also been seen in the proximity of RAF West Freugh, which is used for experimental flight

The Australian Jindivik (Aboriginal for 'the hunted one') jet-powered target drone was designed to a British Ministry of Defence requirement and it is still in service 45 years later. (NAWCWD)

BOSNIA

The civil wars in the former Yugoslavia, which began with the break-away of Slovenia in June 1991, spread through Croatia to Bosnia.

To try to understand what was going on in the region, the United Nations and NATO deployed all of their surveillance assets, including their UAVs.

The first UAV deployed over Bosnia was the Gnat-750 long-endurance UAV which was operated by the CIA from the Croatian island of Hvar in 1993. At the same time French Fox AT1 UAVs supported UNPROFOR from Bihac in Bosnia.

Next to arrive were USMC Pioneers with Task Force Eagle, the US contingent to IFOR, while the Gnat's big brother, Predator, deployed to Albania in July 1995 for a six-month Joint Service operation during which Predators flew 128 missions in support of NATO operations *Deny Flight* and *Deliberate Force.* In a second six-month deployment, USAF Predators operated from the Tazsar in Hungary in support of IFOR.

French CL-289 UAVs have also flown more than 500 IFOR missions from a base at Mostar Airport in Bosnia.

One Fox AT1, two Pioneers and at least three Predators have been lost over Bosnia, most of them due to mechanical failures.

US Marine Corps squadron VMU-1 (home base Yuma, Arizona) equipped with six IAI Pioneer UAVs, at Bovington Airfield, Bosnia, in the winter of 1996. (David Oliver)

A VMU-1 Pioneer lands on the 850 ft strip at Bovington Airfield, using its arrestor hook, after a five-hour mission. The airfield was built on the site of an open-cast coal-mine. (David Oliver)

US Predators at the former secret WarPac base at Taszar operated alongside Hungarian Air Force MiG-21s. One of the three Predators flying IFOR surveillance missions over Bosnia carried the serial number P-007! (Istvan Toperczer)

testing, and Britain's high-security research airfield at Boscombe Down. The UAV, which apparently does not show up on radar, is reported to be coated with new ceramic stealth technologies developed by DERA's Structural Materials Centre, while its exotic propulsion system is based on microwave induction, where the craft rides on radiation shock waves.

The British company AVPRO has also designed a small stealthy reconnaissance UAV, code-named Archangel – a composite-constructed, 15-foot span delta powered by a ducted fan or micro jet engine. Although it is aimed at an RAF requirement, the

Ministry of Defence remains reluctant to commit itself to the acquisition of a capable, state-of-the-art UAV system, or to admit that any are even under development!

CANADA

Canadair's first intelligence-gathering UAV dates back to 1961 with a joint Canada-UK project for the British Army. The result was the CL-89 Midge, a recoverable and reusable drone launched with a booster rocket and powered by a 125 lb thrust turbojet engine. It entered service in the UK in 1969 and was ordered by France and Italy in the early 1970s. Despite having been operational with the British Army for more than 20 years, equipped with only optional cameras and having no real-time data-link transmission, the Midge was the only UAV available to it during the Gulf War, where it was used with some success.

A longer-range, day/night-capable derivative, the CL-289, powered by a 242 lb thrust BMW Rolls-Royce turbojet and having an operational radius of 100 miles, was developed for the German and French armies in the 1980s. Aerospatiale produced a ground-control station for the French CL-289, known as the Pivot, which entered service with the French Army in 1992. Since then the 7th Artillery Regiment from Nevers has used its CL-289, stationed at Mostar airport, to monitor the Bosnian cease-fire under the terms of France's Implementation Force (IFOR) engagement in Bosnia. During its year-long deployment, French CL-289s flew more than 500 IFOR missions.

The Canadian UAV entered service with the German Army in 1990. Seven years later, Dornier (Dasa) was upgrading the system by implementing

Unmanned Canberra U-10 high-flying target drones were tactical bombers converted by Shorts Brothers for use by the RAF and Royal Navy.

Far left
Flight Refuelling's ASAT high-speed, jet-powered drone equipped with JATO for zero-length launching. (FRA)

Left
A Phoenix System on display.

Royal Navy strike Sea Vixens were the last UK fighters to be converted into high-speed unmanned targets, in the 1980s. (Arthur Pearcy)

A pilotless RAF Meteor U-16 target drone, a converted fighter, in flight off the coast of Wales. (Cobham)

CABIN GROUND TEST CONNECTION

Insert top
Both the USAF and the US Navy continue to use unmanned versions of the F-4 Phantom. (Tracor)

Insert below
Multi-coloured un-manned Hellcats at NAS Atlantic City in 1946. They were later used to fly through nuclear-bomb test clouds during Operation Crossroads. (National Archives)

Main Picture
Twenty-eight 'witches on broomsticks' denote the number of unmanned missions flown, without being hit, by this RAF Meteor U-16 based at RAF Llanbedr. (Arthur Pearcy)

The jet-powered, RATO Canadair CL-289 has been in service with the French and German Armies for more than a decade.

a global-positioning system (GPS)-based tracking system and integrating new sensors, including a synthetic aperture radar (SAR) which Dornier is developing with Thomson-CSF.

Canadair's CL-227 Sentinel is a radical change in design from its jet-powered, rocket-launched CL-89/289 UAVs. The company flew a proof of

concept contra-rotating rotary-wing vehicle powered by a Wankel rotary engine in 1978. Nicknamed the Peanut because of its shape, it began as a 3-foot high, 90 lb vertical take-off and landing (VTOL) vehicle that has doubled its size in the 20 years of its development and can now carry a 100 lb payload. Now powered by a 52 shp William's turboshaft, the CL-227 is targeting the lucrative US Navy Maritime VTOL UAV System (MAVUS) shipboard vehicle. Canadair has developed automatic maritime launch and recover equipment for the Sentinel, based on the RAST helicopter-recovery system which features a deck lock to engage the UAV's feet in a grid after landing. The CL-227 is also in competition with the Dornier Seamos for NATO's maritime UAV requirement, and an enhanced version, the CL-427 Puma, came close to winning the US Army's joint tactical UAV competition, running a close second to the Alliant Outrider.

Another Canadian company has recently entered the UAV world by marketing an unmanned version of the Monitor threat-simulation aircraft that is under evaluation by the US Navy. The small, lightweight, composite-constructed, two-seat military trainer is being developed by the Canadian Aerospace Group with the support of the US Sikorsky Aircraft Corporation. This UAV is designed to be powered by a variety of off-the-shelf turbofans in the 3,000 lb thrust class. As an unmanned Monitor, it could carry a useful payload of over 3,000 lb at a speed of 500+ mph and at a range of more than 1,000 miles. By virtue of its composite construction and small size, the Monitor would have excellent survivability in its role as a reconnaissance platform.

Canadair's CL-227 Sea
Sentinel vertical take-off
UAV, nicknamed the
'Peanut', is designed to
be launched and recovered
on a warship's helipad.
(Canadair)

PATHFINDER

Pathfinder is a solar-powered, ultra-lightweight research aircraft developed by AeroVironment Corp. The vehicle will be tested on very high-altitude and extremely long-duration flights lasting several weeks or months.

On 11 September 1995 the aircraft reached an altitude of 50,500 ft setting a new altitude record for a solar-powered aircraft. It made a high-altitude flight on 9 June 1997 from the Pacific Missile Range Facility at Barking Sands, Kauai, Hawaii, and reached an amazing 67,350 ft.

Tests are set to continue for a further few months and some flights will carry a range of environmental research sensors. There are also plans to place a digital camera on board which will be linked via a modem to a ground site which will transmit pictures back directly onto an Internet World Wide Web site.

Funded by the Ballistic Missile Defence Organization (BMDO) as an offshoot of the 'Star Wars' initiative, Pathfinder was conceived as a 'Scud-buster'. Armed with a battery of light-weight, hypervelocity guided missiles and using state-of-the-art sensors, it was to float for days or weeks high above (60,000 ft or more) Scud-launching zones at times of tension. It would then knock down the enemy rockets as they slowly climbed into the high atmosphere.

The obvious problem for a solar-powered plane – what to do when the sun goes down? – was solved by using a sealed cycle hydrogen/oxygen fuel cell that was charged up during the day by excess electricity produced by the solar panels.

The aircraft is controlled by varying the thrust of the engines. Although they produce comparatively little power, they are sufficient to permit Pathfinder to become airborne in the width of a standard runway.

NASA AND CIVILIAN UAVs

During the 1960s and 1970s, the US National Aeronautics and Space Agency (NASA) was involved with a number of highly secret UAV projects, including the cancelled Lockheed D-21 Tagboard with the Central Intelligence Agency (CIA) and the testing of Teledyne Ryan's late-generation Firebees. Following the declassification in 1993 of one of the Skunk Works' 'Blackest' programmes, four stored D-21B surveillance drones were released to NASA as hypersonic test vehicles. To date none of these has yet flown, although NASA also operates some SR-71 Blackbirds which were originally used as a launch vehicle for the ramjet-powered D-21. Another project that NASA inherited this time from the BMDO (Ballistic Missile Defense Organization) was the solar-powered AeroVironment Pathfinder. In 1983 AeroVironment was contracted to build an ultralight, 100 ft wing-span, unmanned aircraft driven by eight solar-powered electric motors, to be used for surveillance. Designed to climb to 75,000 ft and have unlimited loiter time over likely target areas, the aircraft, known as Halsol (High ALtitude SOLar), flew only once before being cancelled in 1987. However, during the Gulf War, the detection of Iraq's Scud intercontinental ballistic missiles became a high priority for Coalition commanders, and in 1992 Halsol was re-evaluated.

As a result, a larger, more powerful version, called Pathfinder, was flown in 1993, which subsequently set altitude records of 50,000 ft and 67,000 ft for a solar-powered aircraft. Its achievement was made public, although the original 'Black' programme that spawned the aircraft was not.

Pathfinder's development was now taken over by

NASA as part of the agency's seven-year Environment Research Aircraft and Sensor Technology (ERAST) programme which plans to have a range of UAVs by the year 2001 to take air samples at different altitudes to monitor pollution and measure ozone levels for environmental research. Pathfinders, which could also be used for telecommunication relays, mapping the earth's surface and monitoring the weather, will circle the globe at between 75,000 and 100,000 ft for months on end.

Other more conventional UAVs under evaluation for ERAST include the medium-endurance Aurora Perseus, a 60 ft wing-span aircraft powered by an 80 hp turbo-charged piston engine, which first flew in 1991. NASA's Perseus A is designed to carry a 992 lb payload for a maximum of 72 hours. The programme met with a setback at the end of 1996 when one of the prototypes broke up in mid-air.

Another ERAST-programme aircraft is the high-altitude atmospheric-research development member of General Atomics' Gnat 750/Predator family of UAVs. Known as Altus, it has extended wings and an engine designed to take it up to about 50,000 ft.

The short-range Sikorsky Cypher environmental-monitoring UAV resembles the original flying saucers first seen in sci-fi B-movies in the 1950s. Its life is provided by a number of short blades which rotate at high speed within the circular body of the aircraft, in a similar way to those in the domestic FlyMo lawn mower. UAV designers are nothing if not innovative.

NASA is sharing some of the UAV technology that it has developed over the past 30 years with US universities, to spread its practical applications to industry. The Carnegie Mellon University in

Pennsylvania is marketing control systems and remote-sensing equipment, including GPS, for a range of small, fully autonomous, unmanned helicopters which can be accurately positioned over their target to within 6 in! The university research department is using the Japanese Yamaha R-50, a 12 ft long, remote-controlled helicopter as a proof-of-concept vehicle that could be used for spraying crops, checking power lines or filming in inaccessible locations where a camera crew could not get to, such as on mountaineering shoots or rapids and white-water sequences. Designed to undertake similar roles is the Schweizer RoboCopter 300, an unmanned derivative of the proven piston-engined 300CB helicopter. Offering a significantly higher payload and greater performance than other unmanned helicopters, the RoboCopter is being developed in conjunction with Kawada Industries of Japan.

The renowned Massachusetts Institute of Technology (MIT) is also involved in UAV research: developing GPS and video camera-guidance systems for precision location and identification of toxic or radioactive substances by robotic aircraft. Such devices would be invaluable in the event of a major chemical or nuclear accident, such as the Bhopal and Chernobyl disasters of the 1980s.

MIT has also turned its attention to avert the effects of global warming. This involves planting new forests by dropping young trees in self-planting cones from the air. Up to 100,000 trees 'bombs' could be planted by a single aircraft, such as a C-130 Hercules, in a day. A Japanese unmanned airship, capable of staying airborne for up to two years, would survey the often-remote locations of the world that would be selected for

The Carnegie Melon University in Pennsylvania is developing practical applications for NASA's UAV technology, using a Japanese Yamaha R-50 UAV helicopter for its trials.

tree-bombing. It would check the area for people, using high-definition cameras and infrared sensors, before the bomb run could commence. The UAV airship would then monitor the growth of the new forest before moving on to a new replant location.

Unmanned airships are also being designed as communications relays, while tethered aerostats are already used for monitoring the environment or drug smugglers. The US Coast Guard and Air Force operate 16 TCOM low altitude surveillance system (LASS) aerostats, carrying high-power, sophisticated radar systems at altitudes from 3,000 to 20,000 ft, to form an unbroken surveillance line across the southern border of the USA and out across the sea to the Bahamas. The aerostats'

The RoboCopter is UAV helicopter being developed by the Japanese company Kawada and Schweizer Aircraft. It can be used for crop-spraying, power-line checks and police surveillance. (Kawada)

ENVIRONMENTAL WARRIORS

Perseus

Designed and built by Aurora Flight Science Corp., Perseus is a propulsion and performance testbed for the ERAST programme. The aircraft is designed to operate in the 65,000 ft region and have a long endurance. Perseus's engine is double turbo-charged to operate in the thin air of the very high environment and has a large and unusually shaped propellor also designed for high altitude.

Seen below, Perseus is being towed into the air by a truck on one of its early trial flights at the vast Edwards AFB complex. Later trials used the aircraft's own engine and a tricycle undercarriage. NASA's Dryden Flight Test Facility nestles alongside the USAF testing operations with the B-1 and B-2 bombers and F-15 and F-16 fighters.

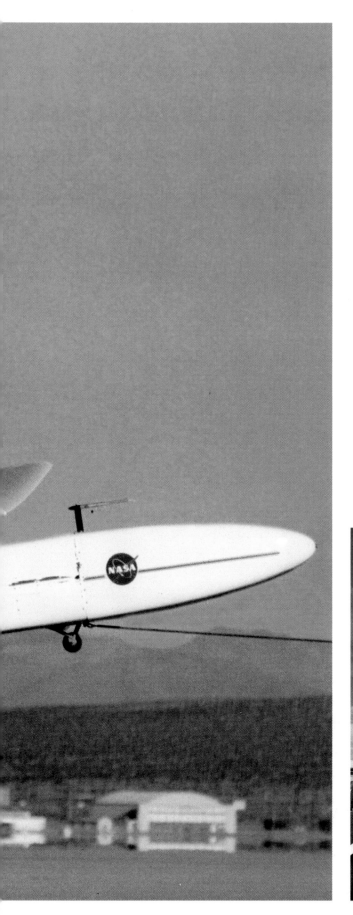

Developed from the military Predator design, Altus has begun to prove itself to be a reliable mid-range work horse. With a new dual turbo-charged engine it will be capable of reaching altitudes beyond 50,000 ft. Previously, in October 1996, Altus set an endurance record for a UAV carrying a science payload. The vehicle spent more than 24 hours at a high altitude during a Department of Energy atmospheric radiation measurement experiment.

TCOM low-altitude surveillance system (LASS) is operated as an anti-drug smuggling asset by the USAF and Coast Guard. They are also used on the Kuwait–Iraq border. (TCOM)

Sikorsky's 'flying saucer': the Cypher multi-mission reconnaissance-and-surveillance UAV.

radars can detect small low-flying aircraft up to 200 miles away. The TCOM maritime aerostat tracking and surveillance system (MATSS) can be mounted on a flatbed trailer, deployed from a ship or towed by a helicopter. Communications with the surface use the latest fibre-optic technology embedded in the umbilical tether.

Designs exist for resurrecting Zeppelin-type ocean-crossing giant airships. However these would not be the luxury passenger airliners of the past, but state-of-the-art unmanned gargantuans capable of lifting heavyweight and unwieldy cargo that would normally be difficult to fit into a ship's hold. These giant UAVs could travel huge distances, navigating and avoiding weather patterns completely autonomously. Other high-speed Jumbo-jet sized UAVs may be used to carry large numbers of small objects, such as letters and parcels. The overnight delivery specialists, such as FedEx, DHL and UPS, presently own and operate large fleets of converted passenger jets in order to carry this lucrative cargo,

and pre-programmed UAVs could become the international aerial post vans of the future.

It is not just the military that need accurate information about a fast-moving and potentially deadly enemy. Firefighters, for whom forest fires are often a daily hazard, are in need of a reconnaissance facility which can watch for hours for the tell-tale wisp of smoke and then focus in on the hotspots to direct water-bombing planes which will hopefully save millions of trees and the investment they represent. Such a system was demonstrated on 8 October 1996 to the US Department of Agriculture Forest Service and the University of Montana at Stevensville, Montana.

The Firebird 2001 remotely controlled UAV, designed and built by Israel Aircraft Industries' (IAI) Malat division, successfully demonstrated that it could deliver real-time, highly accurate data of a fire's size, speed, perimeter and movement. Using GPS technology, geographic information systems (GIS) mapping and forward-looking infrared (FLIR) cameras, firefighters and fire managers will be able to instantly receive dynamic, visual and statistical information about a wildfire. Given this type of continuous information, fire managers will have the potential to control fires faster, keep fires smaller and significantly reduce the risk to firefighters.

Attending the live Firebird demonstration were wild-land fire managers from across the USA and Canada. Representatives from firefighting aircraft companies also had a keen interest in the UAV's capabilities. One of those present, Dan Bailey, Forest Fire Management Officer, Lolo National Forest, Montana, said, 'As we move into the next century in the wild-land fire arena, it is important that we take advantage of new technology that will help us deal with the ever-increasing complexity of wildfire suppression. The use of unmanned aircraft systems in fire surveillance, intelligence-gathering, firefighter safety and cost effectiveness is a step in this direction.'

Boeing produced this high-altitude, long-range, twin-engined UAV, the Condor. The 200 ft wing-span Condor gained the 67,028 ft altitude record for piston-engined aircraft in 1988. (Boeing)

WEIRD AND WONDERFUL

While there has been a huge increase in the potential military and commercial applications of the UAV in the last few years, there has also been an incredible proliferation of UAV designs – anything goes! Tilt-wing, swing-wing, rotor-wing, canard-wing, co-axial, flying-wing, tilt-body, solar-powered, diesel-powered, ramjet-powered, radiation-powered, fanjet-powered, electric-engine powered, rotary engine-powered, microbotics and giant airships.

These are just a few of the diverse designs that have or will become practical UAVs in the next few years. The only limit to unmanned serial vehicle design will be the limit of man's imagination and ingenuity when the UAV comes of age in the next century.

Bell's manoeuvrable tilt-rotor UAV Eagle Eye resembles a scaled-down version of its V-22 Osprey. The Eagle Eye is capable of fulfilling numerous military and civil roles. (Bell Boeing)

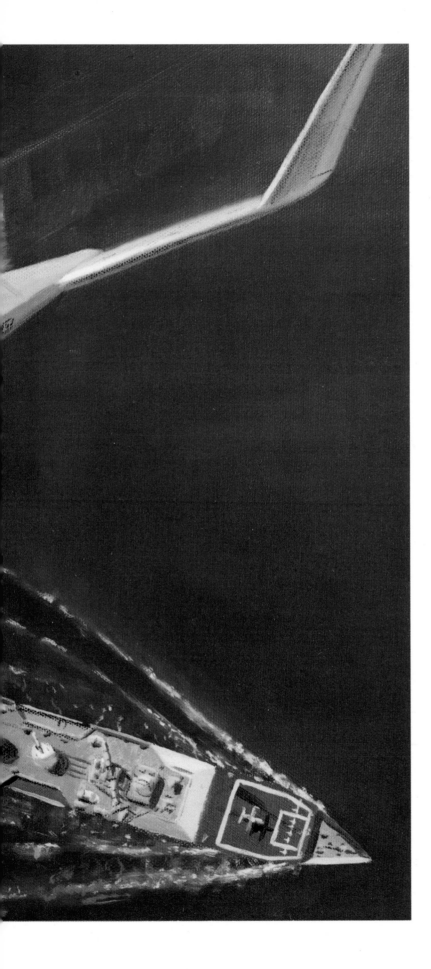

Another innovative UAV design is the MDH Canard Rotor/Wing which performs as a rotary-wing aircraft for take-off and hover, and as a fixed-wing aircraft for high-speed cruise. (McDonnell Douglas Helicopters)

In the world of military projects acronyms and strange-sounding names abound. Of these the most recent is called the Tier projects. Tier is an Advanced Research Projects Agency (ARPA) 'procurement' project name: official military designations are assigned later. The main objective of ARPA projects is to develop and manufacture the systems using the 'Section 845 – Other Agreements Authority' granted by

Congress. This permits ARPA, now called the Defense Advanced Research Projects Agency (DARPA), to develop solutions for military problems, outside of the burden of normal defence-procurement channels, so as to speed up the use of advanced technology.

DARPA is essentially a group of scientists and project managers who push technology to its practical limit to get results for various US agencies. Chief among the organizations with which DARPA has close links are the ever-secret Central Intelligence Agency, CIA, and the more public Defense Airborne Reconnaissance Office (DARO).

TIER I – THE CIA CARRIES THE TORCH

General Atomics Aeronautical: Gnat 750

Although it is not officially acknowledged, the Tier 1 Gnat 750 was procured by the CIA. If this seems unusual, it is because it was in response to an unusual and fast-developing problem: how to get widespread coverage about what was happening in the former Yugoslavia without going to the expense of using what are euphemistically called 'national assets' – spy satellites and high-altitude

reconnaissance aircraft. Designed for high-intensity conflicts, the national assets were not capable of providing the close-up details of a widespread, low-intensity civil war. In a very short period of time, General Atomics Aeronautical – which had come into the UAV business when it bought out a company called Leading Systems – developed the Gnat 750 from a project originally named Amber 1. What the CIA got was a tactical-reconnaissance/surveillance UAV optimized to their requirements, which were: an endurance of 24 to 30 hours at 5,000 to 15,000 ft with a relatively small 140 lb, state-of-the-art electro-optical (EO) payload.

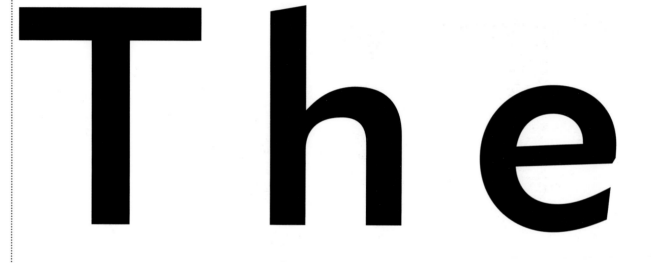

Exact numbers are difficult to confirm, but at least two were bought by the CIA at first. One crashed at the El Mirage, California, test facility and another one is believed to be leased, together with a ground station. An early priority was to extend the communications range of the aircraft.

To this end, a small number of two-seat Schweizer RG-8A Condor aircraft, which had previously been owned by the USCG, was used as an

Tier PROJECTS

intermediate data-relay aircraft. A later development was to attach a dome to the back of the aircraft which contained a satellite aerial.

For obvious reasons, little has been revealed of their operational use, but we do know that, using mostly contractor-supplied and -trained personnel, the CIA carried out almost continuous over-flights of the hotspot areas of Yugoslavia. The base for this was Gjadar, in neighbouring Albania, which was leased for a sum of money and for an undisclosed period of time (it is thought that they were also deployed from Croatia). The intelligence supplied by this small support team was of key value in helping to develop the peace process.

Reports speculate about four more aircraft and a ground station having been procured. These aircraft have supposedly been updated with the Predator-type engine.

The Gnat 750 has also been ordered by Turkey and has apparently seen operations in northern Iraq, but this may or may not be simply a cover for CIA operations. However, confirmation of Tier activity in Iraq did slip out at a recent UAV conference. The secret world of UAVs is alive and well today and operates from one of the many CIA facilities in Langley, Virginia.

PREDATOR

The first of the USAF's 'Dream Team' of high-tech UAVs, the General Atomics Predator was developed from its Gnat 750, originally a CIA 'black' programme. Officially known as Tier II Medium Altitude Endurance (MAE) UAV, Predator first flew in July 1994. After trials at the remote UAV training centre at Fort Huachuca in Arizona, it flew in a Special Operations exercise in June 1995 before deploying to Albania and later to Hungary where it flew US joint service surveillance missions over Bosnia.

Predator conducted a number of exercises with US Navy warships including a Carrier Battle Group, and a nuclear-powered submarine during which it acted as the 'eyes' of a SEAL team which was landed from the submarine for a covert mission ashore.

As from September 1996 US Predators came under the command of USAF's 11th Reconnaissance Squadron based at Indian Springs Air Force Auxiliary Field, of the Nellis AFB complex situated in the Nevada Desert.

UNCLASSIFIED

Predator MAE UAV
TESAR Training Flight Imagery

C–12 Beechcraft
Occupying Aircraft Shelter

29 JAN 96
Altitude: 16,417 ft
Slant Range: 29,912 ft
Swath Width: 936 ft

UNCLASSIFIED

Insert
SAR imagery 'looking' through a hanger roof.

Developed from the Gnat 750 in 1994, Predator demonstrated its ability to support carrier battle-groups during exercises, when the submarine USS *Chicago* controlled the UAV and received its down-link images. (General Atomics)

Predator was deployed in July 1995 to Albania and to Taszar, in Hungary, to conduct surveillance missions over Bosnia in support of IFOR. Taszar is shown here, from where Predator flew 850 hours and 128 missions in its six-month deployment. (Istvan Toperczer)

A Predator Tier II medium-altitude endurance (MAE) UAV, belonging to the USAF 11th Reconnaissance Squadron, landing at its base at Indian Springs in the Nevada Desert. (Tim Gerlach)

TIER II – FROM BOSNIA WITH LOVE

General Atomics Aeronautical Systems Inc.: Predator

Predator, also known as the medium altitude endurance (MAE) UAV or Tier II, is a derivative of the Gnat 750 UAV and is destined to be the Pentagon's joint-service UAV. The Predator's 44 hp engine gives it an endurance of up to 40 hours and a cruising altitude of 25,000 ft with a 450 lb payload, including a hi-tech synthetic aperture radar (SAR); which put in layman's language means it can survey up to 1,300 nautical square miles.

The first flight was on 7 March 1994, and ten UAVs, three ground stations and sensor systems were delivered for $31.7 million – other sources have quote $3 million per UAV, including the sensor package.

Initial tests were flown from Fort Huachuca, Arizona, with EO and IR cameras and line-of-sight (LOS) data links – and some are now fitted with satellite data links for OTH (Over the Horizon) flights.

They participated with great success in Roving Sands, a combined-theatre, ballistic-missile defence and integrated air-defence exercise, lasting from April to May 1995, based at Fort Bliss, Texas, and the White Sands Missile Range, New Mexico, searching over a four-state area in a hunt for Scud-type mobile missiles. This was one of the problem missions during operation Desert Storm.

Predator was deployed in July 1995, allegedly alongside Albanian-based CIA Gnat 750s, for use in Bosnia. Two were lost in quick succession, the first being on 11 August 1995 (reports say it was shot down by Bosnian Serb forces, but this is being reconsidered). Another one was intentionally destroyed by flying it into a mountainside just three days later, because it developed engine trouble at the end of an operational mission. The press reports of these incidents were almost non-existent compared to the shoot-down of Capt. Scott O'Grady during the same period.

Despite some early limitations for all-weather operation, Predator helped to determine the course of the Bosnia conflict. During September 1995, after several diplomatic and operational initiatives to relieve shelling and intimidation of civilian enclaves, especially in Bosnia's Sarajevo–Gorazde area, NATO forces resorted to active bombing to bring the warring factions to the negotiating table. Many previous agreements to remove field weapons from the area had been broken, but NATO forces could not hold the violators responsible without confirmation. With Predator, however, weapons movements became subject to long-dwell video surveillance, and continuous coverage of roads showed no evidence of weaponry being withdrawn. This UAV resource thus gave NATO commanders the key piece of intelligence that underlay their decision to resume the bombing campaign which, in turn, led to the Dayton peace accord signed in December 1995.

November 1995 saw Predator's return to the USA from Albania. Poor weather and severe icing conditions had been reducing its effectiveness. A new capability was added to its list. An SAR sensor was installed under its nose, just ahead of the sensor turret. This gave the ability to see through clouds, rain, snow and, on occasion, the thin roofs of storage buildings. IR cameras had defeated the night – SAR defeated the weather! With the satellite links in their bulbous noses, Predators could send this imagery through the Ku-band SATCOM (Satellite Communications)

IMAGERY

A Picture is worth a Thousand Words...The Magic of Imagery

Fascinating aircraft like Global Hawk, DarkStar or Predator exist purely to give a US or Allied commander an image of the battle-field. These aircraft use a whole range of imaging techniques, some of which are commercially available off the shelf while others are definitely state of the art.

Global Hawk and DarkStar use two forms of sensor, electro-optical and Synthetic Aperture Radar, SAR. The optical systems share one set of reflective optics, essentially a high-powered telescope for collecting the light, be it visual or infrared. Although unconfirmed, this system is probably similar to the most modern equipment on the manned Lockheed U-2 spyplane.

Similarily the SAR is a developed version of that found in the U-2. In addition to being able to look through clouds, SAR can check to see if any of the radar return have moved and figure out the speed of the movement. This ability is called MTI (Moving Target Indicator) and requires extremely powerful computers.

MTI allows a battlefield commander to look for large movements of trucks or tanks and thereby see the direction of enemy movements. Alternatively, it can also help in the search for lone vehicles, such as SCUD missile launchers.

With so much information from these sensors the problem is now information overload!

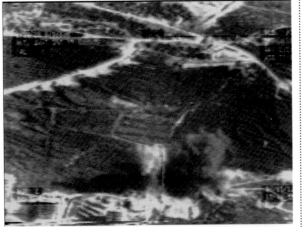

Searchers videoed bombing and shelling in the Baker Valley.

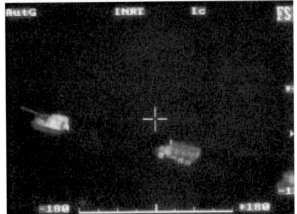

Infrared images of tanks on the move.

Main picture
A Bosnian arms dump taken by a UAV.

Taken by a Firebee this anti-aircraft artillery site was soon to become another target in the Vietnamese conflict.

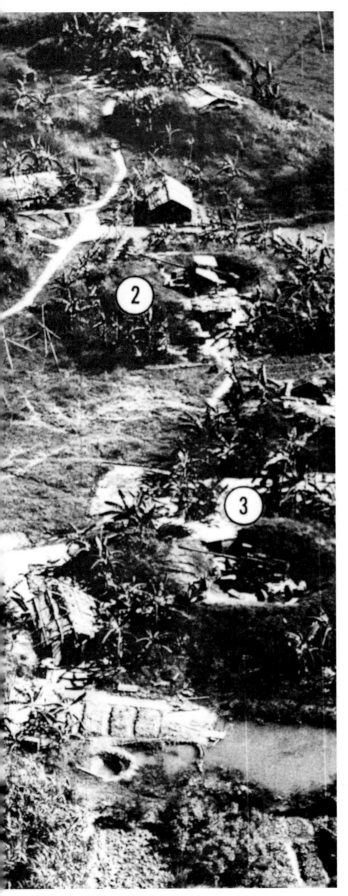

Electro Optical magnifications of a Bosnian arms dump.

With infrared, the night no longer belongs to 'Charlie or Ivan'.

Predator provided pictures of street demonstrations in Bosnia during the elections.

The 27 ft wing-span Predator, the USAF's first operational UAV, is powered by a turbo-charged Rotax piston engine. It can carry EO sensors and SAR for up to 40 hours at a maximum height of 25,000 ft. (Tim Gerlach)

link. To warn against icing conditions, ice-sensing features were added to enable poor weather operation.

Predators were re-deployed in March 1996 to Taszar, Hungary, to continue supporting NATO operations in Bosnia. A further aircraft was damaged in what was said to be the first-ever crash landing that was controlled via a satellite. Landing in a ploughed field, the nose gear broke when it dropped into a ditch, but the airframe and its sensors were recovered in good condition; so good, in fact, that the operators were able to spot the rescue team before they saw the Predator, and so they guided the team to it for the pick-up – another first perhaps?

As to the success of the Predators, the quotation below from a DARO publication says it all:

UAV deployments to Bosnia, in support of joint and combined operations, are the major UAV success story of Financial Year 1996. They include both operational triumphs and acquisition lessons learned. Principally, they illustrate how UAVs can contribute vital information to enhance tactical operations and strategic decision-making.

US-based Predators have demonstrated their prowess in a number of exercises, including one with the US Customs Service (autumn 1995), a US Navy carrier battle group (autumn 1995) and, very impressively, with a US Navy nuclear-powered submarine (spring 1996). In this mission the Predator took off from an airfield, then flight and sensor control passed to the sub, which used it to track the success of a special forces SEAL team which it dispatched on a simulated covert mission – helping in the destruction of an enemy mobile missile site. The imagery which the Predator returned in near-real-time had all the spooky elements of a Tom Clancy novel. With the Predator's help, the SEAL commander in the submerged submarine was able to direct his men to and from the target in the way which best avoided enemy patrols.

On 30 June 1996, Predator completed its 30-

month ACTD. On 26 July, General Atomics received a $23 million contract for a further five UAVs and ancillary equipment. Another important event in the Predator world happened on 2 September 1996. The Air Force Air Combat Command's 11th Reconnaissance Squadron, at Nellis Air Force Base, Nevada, assumed operational control of the aircraft and its equipment. It was a historical occasion – the first-ever USAF UAV squadron. This unit uses the Nellis Air Force Base Satellite airfield at Indian Springs, which is on the edge of the test facility known as Area-51. This may be significant in that Area-51 is associated with unconfirmed top-secret UAV projects. In future, the 11th Reconnaissance Squadron may also operate the US Air Force DarkStar and Global Hawk aircraft.

In the Defense Appropriations Act for the financial year 1997, Congress transferred Predator production funding from the Defence-wide Procurement account to the Navy's Procurement account and increased the amount by $50 million to $115.8 million.

Other needs on the Predator wish list include a more robust communication link throughput; improved data dissemination to better exploit the near-real-time imagery products; the ability for UAV pilots to talk directly to air traffic control agencies, and a full IFF capability. Most of this is now in hand.

Some of the additional highlights of the second Predator deployment include:

- Routine flight in congested airspace, across two national boundaries; control by AWACS in operations area.
- Passed video imagery to Joint STARS ground

station module in Hungary – first UAV-Joint STARS inter-operation.
- During late summer/early autumn 1996, monitored mass grave sites near Sarajevo, which provided evidence of 1,995 deaths.
- September 1996: monitored the Bosnia election activities.
- Quick-response observations to preclude confrontations between Bosnia actions or with NATO units.
- October 1996: covering and monitoring of deploying forces.

Even more significant than the Predator performance 'firsts' is the wide use made of its imagery both in-theatre and back in the USA. The dissemination capability means that the image, which is in digital form, is sent to a commercial communications satellite, such as the Intelsat 602. From space it is transmitted simultaneously to three locations:

1 Back to the Predator control station for the sensor operator to see what his/her camera is pointing at.
2 Back to a Trojan Spirit communications terminal mounted on a truck. From here it is distributed to various military/political clients 'in country', including the commanders in the field.
3 Back to a classified communications station in Britain, from where it is passed via an optical-fibre cable to Washington, DC, and thence around the military network.

Using the SATCOM-based Joint Broadcast System (JBS), the US services have, in effect, the military equivalent to CNN. For the first time,

GLOBAL HAWK

A product of one of the world's most successful UAV manufacturers, Teledyne Ryan, Global Hawk represents the pinnacle of 20th-century UAV technology.

The Tier II Plus High-Altitude Endurance (HAE) Global Hawk completes the DARPA 'dream team' of surveillance UAVs that is planned to give the USAF an unassailable lead in intelligence-gathering in the next century.

The quantum leap in Global Hawk's capability in the late 1990s can only be compared with the U-2 in the 1960s.

The 116ft wing-span composite-constructed Global Hawk is designed to fly from a base in the United States, fly autonomously to a country of interest, loiter at a speed of 400 mph and a height of 65,000 ft for 24 hours while transmitting surveillance data, and then return to its base without refuelling.

Diagram
The 116 ft wing-span Global Hawk, powered by a 7,644 lb thrust Allison AE 3007H turbofan, can carry a hefty 2,000 lb payload of synthetic aperture radar (SAR) and EO and infra-red (IR) sensors. (Teledyne Ryan)

Final assembly of the first Teledyne Ryan Global Hawk UAV. Note the assembly workers, which give scale to the aircraft.

The high-altitude endurance (HAE) Global Hawk Tier III Plus built by UAV specialists Teledyne Ryan. It is scheduled to make its first flight in 1997. (Rick Spurway)

Right
The 7,600 lb thrust Allison turbofan being installed in Global Hawk prior to its first flight.

Far right
The 'low-burn' engine will enable Global Hawk to loiter at 340 mph for 24 hours!

the Predator–JBS network provided for the simultaneous broadcast of live UAV video to more than 15 users, showing a common picture of the 'battlefield'. The video imagery can be viewed either as full-motion video or via a 'mosaicking' technique at the ground station.

THE DYNAMIC DUO – GLOBAL HAWK AND DARKSTAR

Global Hawk, also known as the Conventional High Altitude Endurance (CONV HAE) or Tier II+ UAV, is intended as one part of a dynamic duo of UAVs. It represents the workhorse element for missions requiring long-range deployment, of 14,000 miles or more, and wide-area surveillance, or for a mission which requires a protracted parking above or close to a target area. So that it does not generate political embarrassment for local friendly nations who wish to offer airfield facilities, it is able to fly directly from well outside the theatre of operation while still providing extended mission time. It is not intended for use over high threat areas, but with its heavy payload of state-of-the-art EO/IR and SAR sensors, it can stand off a considerable distance, much like the manned U-2 does, while still providing both wide-area and spot imagery from very high altitude. Operating from 65,000 ft, twice the height of a commercial airliner, and equipped with effective jamming and hi-tech decoys, simulations have shown that it is difficult, but not impossible, to shoot down. Stealth technology would make it safer still, but this would reduce the payload and, more importantly, make it many times more expensive to buy and operate.

Powered by a single Rolls-Royce Allison turbofan engine which is in widespread commercial use, its striking characteristic is its wing-span which, at 114 ft, is greater than a Boeing 737 airliner. The bulbous nose, which contains a 48 inch satellite antennae, is similar to that carried on the venerable U-2 spy plane. This connection into space is very high speed and provides either highly detailed video or still pictures to the world-wide US military network.

Like its DarkStar cousin, Global Hawk is not only unmanned but it has been designed from the outset to be an autonomous aircraft. The most obvious difference that this makes is not on the aircraft but in the control centre: there are no pilot positions with a joystick or pedals or throttle, just mission-planner positions. These operators tell Global Hawk where they would like it to go and what they are interested in looking at; the rest of the equation is worked out by Global Hawk on its own. The computer-power of Global Hawk is greater than any other UAV.

Global Hawk has a massive 116 ft wing, which is made of a high-tech, light-weight, composite material.

In following the concept that Global Hawk was one element of combined recce facility, it was decided that the control centre, called the Common Ground Segment (CGS), will also be capable of launching and recovering its unusual-looking counterpart, the Lockheed–Martin/Boeing DarkStar.

calmed by the time DarkStar touched down at the end of its 40-minute flight.

DarkStar has a flatish circular body which houses a deeply buried FJ-44 turbofan engine, along with the sensors and all ancillary computers and 'black boxes' that keep it flying. The wings are made from lightweight carbon fibre and contain

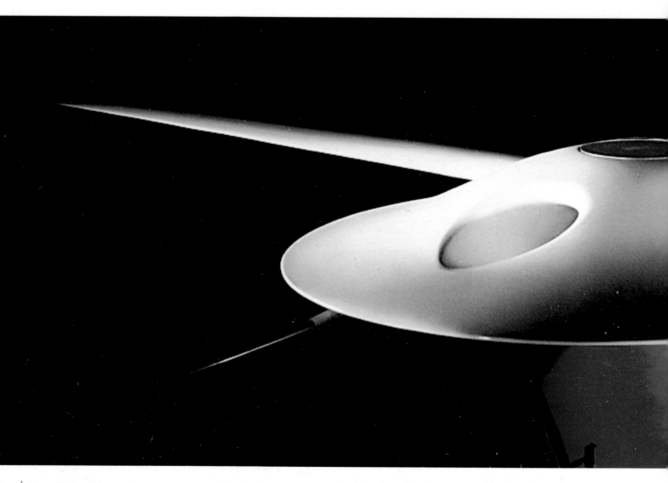

Tier III – (Minus)
Lockheed–Martin/Boeing DarkStar

When DarkStar took to the air in March 1996 it became one of the strangest-looking flying machines in the history of aviation. Even its test-flight manager described it as 'a clamshell with wings'; but to many of the Californian inhabitants below its flight-test route it looked just like a flying saucer, and they phoned the police to tell them about it! Visions of an alien invasion were

the fuel. The whole of the aircraft shape is designed to make it invisible to a tracking radar, quiet to the ear and with a cool heat signature – the basic building blocks of what is know as 'stealth'. The exterior, and probably key parts of the interior too, are coated with a paint that absorbs radar energy. The underneath of the body and wing is painted natural flat black, while a shiny white finish keeps the topside cooler.

The DarkStar's degree of stealthiness is greater

than either the F-117A Stealth Fighter (another Lockheed Skunk Works design) or the B-2 Spirit Stealth Bomber. This is because whereas its stealthy cousins are designed for a quick single-pass strike, DarkStar will have to orbit over a given location for up to eight hours, hence it will stand a greater chance of being spotted. DarkStar's

nodding of its rounded nose was becoming more pronounced. This continued and increased in severity until the plane took off violently and the nose became almost vertical before sliding back earthwards. The starboard wing hit the runway first, flames erupted and pall of sooty smoke rose into the clear desert air. The DarkStar team were

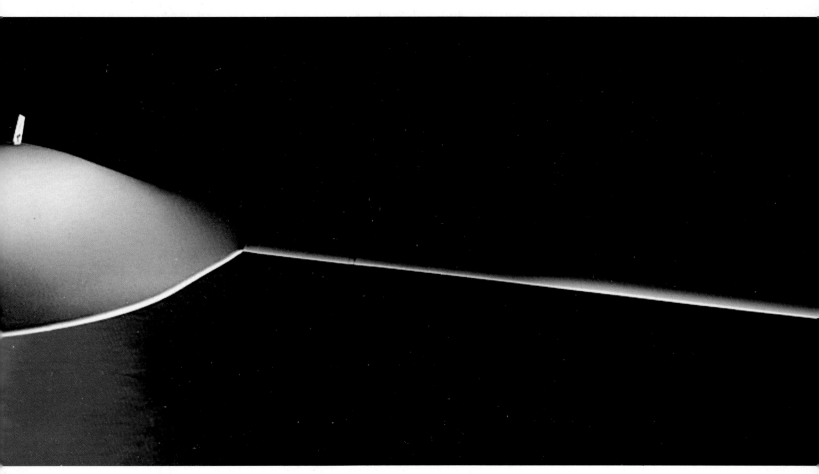

manufacturers would probably have liked it to have been invisible to the naked eye if only for its second flight. The start of the take-off run looked good. The aircraft was towed out by a truck and positioned on the centreline of the runway at Edwards Air Force Base. Last-minute checks were made and the engine spooled-up. The brakes were released and the craft began to move, but something was definitely not right. By the time DarkStar had built up 50 knots plus, a slight

shocked, but no one was hurt.

A crash-investigation team swung into action and included people from outside the project, like Jenny Baer-Reidhart, head of the local NASA Dryden ERAST programme. The salvaged aircraft was examined in detail, with more of it surviving than was apparent at the time of the accident. The remains were then placed in a steel container and its doors were sealed and welded shut. The crash and subsequent fire had apparently made some

The high-altitude, stealthy, Tier III Minus DarkStar UAV is another product of Lockheed Martin's Skunk Works. This one is destined to become one the USAF's fleet of three hi-tech surveillance UAVs early in the next century. (Lockheed Skunk Works)

DARKSTAR

Yet another product of Lockheed's famous 'Skunk Works' at Burbank, California, the Lockheed Martin Boeing DarkStar medium-range endurance UAV is the second, known as Tier III Minus, of USAF's Defense Advanced Research Projects Agency (DARPA) trio of hi-tech surveillance UAVs designed for the 21st century.

The stealthy flying wing design powered by a lightweight Williams FJ-44 turbofan buried in the futuristic body shape, will enable DarkStar to fly undetected at 45,000 ft in all weathers transmitting close-up images to battle-fields working with AWACS and J-STARS.

Despite the crash of the first DarkStar prototype on its second flight in April 1996, a second UAV is scheduled to fly before the end of 1997 and the programme is still set to continue.

It is planned for up to twenty DarkStars to be operated by Air Combat Command's 11th Reconnaissance Squadron, which is based at Indian Springs, Nevada, by the year 2015.

After making its successful first flight from Edwards Air Force Base in March 1996, DarkStar crashed on its second flight in April. A second prototype is due to fly in 1997. (Lockheed Martin Skunk Works)

DarkStar aglow! DarkStar No. 2 illuminated by high-pressure sodium lights while undergoing radar cross-section (RCS) testing to identify its 'hot spots'. (Lockheed Martin Skunk Works)

The futuristic DarkStar, powered by a lightweight Williams FJ44 fan-jet, can carry a 1,250 lb sensor payload over a range of 575 miles, cruising at 45,000 ft. (Lockheed Martin Skunk Works)

Seen in secret hangar in Skunk Work in Palmdale, California, the DarkStar is having its electronic systems tested.

The circular antenna on top of DarkStar is a hi-tech satellite aerial. A similar design will soon be available on wide body jets for receiving TV, phone and Internet signals.

exotic structure, probably the anti-radar coating, toxic. The DarkStar coffin was then buried at an undisclosed site within the Edwards Air Force Base boundary.

The subsequent investigation found that the primary causes of the accident were changes made to the flight-control software, combined with a problem about take-off techniques. Because DarkStar is aerodynamically unstable, it is maintained in controlled flight by a series of computers. It was discovered that between the first and second flight changes had been made to the software programs to correct a small fault. This software was then tested by another piece of software. But the basis of the testing software also had a problem. In this case two wrongs did not make a right. Alterations have since been implemented in the software and changes have been proposed for the wing shape and undercarriage to make the vehicle easier to take off and land. Funding, which

initially stood at $124 million, has been extended to allow for the purchase of an additional prototype.

The crash also caused delays for other aircraft, such as Global Hawk and the X-36, as customers and contractors went through the software and other elements with a fine-toothed comb.

All being well, DarkStar will fly again in the autumn of 1997. The second prototype is in a series of ongoing tests at Lockheed's classified Helendale facility.

It is hoped that eventually up to 20 vehicles could be procured, and probably operated by the Air Combat Command's (ACC) newly established 11th Reconnaissance Squadron (RS) at Nellis Air Force Base, Nevada, which will be based at Indian Springs Air Force Base, inside the restricted zone adjacent to Area-51.

GOODBYE TO THE FIGHTER PILOT?

There is no more complicated flying job than

A US Navy QF-4N Phantom which was used in 'Top Gun' dogfights with Ryan UAVs. (US Navy)

Many USAF BQM-34F fighter UAVs could outfly the latest F-16/F-15 fighters. One, named 'Old Red', survived 82 dogfights. (Ryan)

a fighter pilot's. Your enemy, which may be multiple bogies, has the ability to manoeuvre in three dimensions and at very high speed, your weapons can only be launched within a specific flight envelope, and you may be on the verge of losing consciousness because of pulling high Gs. It has, therefore, been the most challenging job for the unmanned-aircraft designers and engineers to construct a plane with the ability and intelligence to replace the skill of the fighter pilot. Indeed, until recently, there has not been the motivation to take the pilot out of the cockpit. However, propulsion and aerodynamic advances, along with the vastly increasing power of computers and software, have altered this. For the first time ever, manned-aircraft designers are engineering their future fighters with a cockpit that stays firmly on the ground.

The story begins, ironically enough, in the spring of 1971 with a US Navy unit known as Top Gun, which taught dog-fighting skills to naval aviators then engaged with MiGs over Vietnam. The unmanned aircraft in question was the ubiquitous Firebee; not just any old Firebee, but one designed to give the 'best of the best' a real test. The Ryan targets were upgraded with a system dubbed MASTACS (manoeuvrability augmentation system for tactical air combat simulation), and the pilots of Top Gun were keen to prove their superiority.

Bill Wagner, in his book *Fireflies and other Reconnaissance Drones*, takes up the story:

The Weapons School at the NAS Miramar in San Diego was greatly interested in the potential of the elusive bird. Consequently, a graduation exercise was scheduled for May 10 at Pt Mugu, Cdr John C. Smith, commanding officer of the Top Gun school, elected to ride as radar operator and chief tactician as he and three other combat veterans from Vietnam scrambled in F-4 Phantom fighters from Miramar. Both planes were equipped with mixed loads of Sidewinder infrared and Sparrow radar-guided missiles.

What developed was a no-holds-barred contest. Cdr John Pitzen, Top Gun combat instructor, was tactical director for the Firebee, and instructed TRA's Al Donaldson, who manned the remote control station. In effect, they were in the 'cockpit' of the target, and after the stage was set for a head-on approach, the Firebee proved to be an extremely elusive aggressor. Open-circuit radio chatter told of the manned aircraft difficulties. Smith called 'Tally-ho, off the left wing' but the drone was able to pull such a high-G turn that the F-4 could not follow the manoeuvre. Smith was learning the hard way that Donaldson and Pitzen could rack the Firebee into a hundred degree bank and make a 180 degree reversal turn in only 12 seconds, permitting the drone to get in behind the now vulnerable F-4. In this position, the drone ceased being a target, but an attack aircraft.

Ryan BQM-34F fighter UAVs could pull high G manoeuvres. They were used by the US Navy's Top Gun school and at the annual USAF William Tell shooting competition. (Ryan)

The flight was a convincing demonstration of both offensive and defensive manoeuvring by the drone. By going a step beyond the requirements for just a training target, Pandora's box was opened for a quick peek at a potential all-robot Air Force. No comment was made at Mugu concerning the hypothetical case: If the Firebee had been armed with its own missiles, could Pitzen have shot down the Phantoms? Both the Navy and Teledyne Ryan quietly backed away from pushing the concept any further at that time.

HiMAT – NASA's Technology Tester

While the US services were not keen to explore the unmanned-fighter technology, NASA had no problems with this concept, particularly when it could provide a means of testing a whole raft of fighter-related technologies without the danger of losing a pilot. It was also helpful that the programme would cost a fraction of a manned equivalent.

HiMAT (highly manoeuvrable aircraft technology) was essentially what the fighter designers at Rockwell International believed a future fighter

NASA used the Rockwell HiMat high-speed UAV to explore the outer limits of manoeuvrability which no pilot could withstand. (NASA)

plane would look like. Using advanced materials, aerodynamics and computer control in place of a pilot, they could make it less than a third of the size. This sub-scale research vehicle, two examples of which were built, was flown at NASA's Dryden Flight Research Center, Edwards Air Force Base, California, from mid- 1979 to January 1983. It demonstrated not only a range of advanced fighter-aircraft technologies, but also the aerodynamic properties that exist in what is called the transonic realm. The air passing over an aircraft wing behaves differently at sub- and supersonic speeds. This was well understood at the time, but little work had been done on what happens to a wing which bumps along the sonic boundary. This was a problem, because fighter aircraft were beginning to use this speed range to a great extent in the course of combat situations.

In today's world, computer simulations would provide the answers, but in the late 1970s and early 1980s computing power was not up to the job; instead a real-world experiment was required. To make life even more complicated, the wings of future fighters would have to be constructed from a new, lighter, stronger and stiffer material called carbon fibre. Although today it is an everyday product used widely in such things as tennis racquets, carbon fibre was a new material then and required extensive testing in the turbulent transonic realm.

Two vehicles were used in the research programme conducted jointly by NASA and the Air Force Flight Dynamics Laboratory, Wright-Patterson Air Force Base, Ohio. (They also provided data on the use of shape-changing wings and the close-coupled canards now used on many fighter aircraft. Another technology flown on HiMAT were winglets which were vertical or near-vertical wings at the end of each wing-tip. Although they were found to have little use on fighters, theses winglets were found to make the wing more efficient and they can now be seen on most business and commercial jets.)

The two HiMAT vehicles were flown a total of 26 times during the three and a half year programme. On each flight they were carried aloft under the wing of a huge B-52 bomber to 45,000 ft, where the HiMAT's little jet engine was started and they were dropped. Then a test pilot on the ground, still wearing the traditional orange jump-suit, took control of the aircraft for the rest of the flight, with the help of a rather grainy TV camera in the nose and a bank of instruments. As an alternative, a two-seat TF-104 Starfighter also carried back-up controls. Landing was fairly conventional, but instead of having wheels, the HiMAT had metal skids with wooden runners which saved weight. Since it landed on the dry Lake at Edwards – still used by the Space Shuttle – this was not a problem.

What these little aircarft achieved was astonishing! They demonstrated twice the manoeuvrability of the current and projected range of manned fighters. It simply would have been impossible to shoot one down in air-to-air combat.

But there were problems with a project that pushed available technology as far as HiMAT did. Most of them resulted from computers lacking enough power for the job. The power of a laptop today would have filled a large air-conditioned room in the mid to late 1970s, and HiMAT was one of the first computer-controlled aircraft with a digital fly-by-wire control system. Pilot commands were fed to an on-board computer which sent electrical commands to the flight-control surfaces. Therefore, all the computing power could not be placed on board the aircraft, and a lot of it remained on the ground. This created difficulties, with the datalink becoming a critical element.

Both the HiMAT aircraft survived the programme. One of them is located at Dryden. The other belongs to the National Air and Space Museum, Smithsonian Institution in Washington, DC.

X-36 – SON OF HiMAT

One of the technologies which was to have been tested by the HiMAT project was the use of thrust vectoring in combat manoeuvres. Although the nozzle was built, this was never tested in flight. One of the aims of the modern equivalent of HiMAT, the McDonnell Douglas/NASA X-36, is

to explore this very concept.

Just as HiMAT looked the very epitome of the 1980s fighter, with its highly swept wings and canards, so the X-36 looks like a 1990s fighter, still with canards, but also with the angular shapes of stealth and, most noticeable of all, no vertical tail. The thrust vectoring and advanced computer-controlled fly-by-wire technology make it redundant. This may not seem like such a revolutionary idea when one remembers that the rather larger B-2 Spirit Stealth Bomber also has no tail, but it is not meant to manoeuvre like a fighter, while the X-36 most certainly is!

To save money – only $17 millions is being spent on the two X-36 craft and the programme – the aircraft has a wheeled landing gear and will

Taking to the air for the first time, the X-36 proves that a tail is not needed.

take off and land under its own power. As a precaution, it is a little known fact that there is also a parachute tucked inside the aircraft in the event that control might be lost.

Thrust vectoring has been tried on a number of trial aircraft, but just two projects have made it into production – the Anglo-American Harrier and the Russian Yak-38, NATO code-name, Forger. In both of them, the vectoring has been used to give an element of vertical take-off and landing. The X-36 will not be attempting this; instead it will explore the post-stall and low-speed high angle-of-attack realm where the flow of air over the wings loses its power to manoeuvre the aircraft. Manned aircraft, such as the Sukhoi Su-37, the F-15 S/MD Eagle, the AVEN-powered F-16

and the impressive US/German X-31, have explored this concept, but none without the aid of a tail. This statement may be disputed by the X-31 team and particularly by its project manager, Col. Mike Francis. This is because, although the tail physically stayed firmly attached to the aircraft, the fly-by-wire software negated its control effect on the

The size of air vehicles can be gauged from this image as the second X-36 is unpacked for a pre-flight examination at NASA's Dryden facility. Although flown from Dryden, the X-36 is a NASA Ames and McDonnell Douglas project.

A PRESENT-DAY HIMAT

There is no doubt that the X-36 programme has learned from many of the lessons of the HiMAT effort. Whereas HiMAT was complex in its systems the X-36 has gone for robust but simple solutions. One of these is not to have redundancy. Should anything go wrong and the pilot lose control an emergency parachute can be deployed which will bring the X-36 down to earth at a rate that its landing can withstand. It also take off under its own power unlike the HiMAT which had to be carried aloft by a B52.

vehicle. But this experiment was short lived, due to a lack of cash and the crash of one of the two aircraft involved.

There may be other secret test objectives for the X-36, concerned perhaps with the reduced radar return that comes from not having a vertical tail, but we can only guess at what they may be.

MISSION IMPOSSIBLE – THE MICRO UAV?

In 1998 a 12–18 in micro UAV will fly. It will carry a small video camera which weighs 5 gr. Three years later a humming-bird size version will take to the air. Three years after that an insect-sized UAV will lift off with a 1 gr. camera and a 2 gr. pheromone scent detector. Its job will be to enter buildings, find specific humans and watch them. Perhaps, as one engineer suggested, it may even carry a deadly poison in a sting.

This is science *fact* not fiction.

The organization tasked with pulling together the technology to make the micro UAV a reality is the Defense Advanced Research Projects Agency (DARPA). The mission statement for DARPA is interesting in that it is to 'help maintain U.S. technological superiority and guard against unforeseen technological advances by potential adversaries. Consequently, the DARPA mission is to develop imaginative, innovative and often high-risk research ideas offering a significant technological impact that will go well beyond the normal evolutionary developmental approaches; and to pursue these ideas from the demonstration of technical feasibility through the development of prototype systems.' The micro UAV certainly fits into this category.

Engineers are known for their sense of humour

The light weight, electric powered Pointer was used in Desert Storm by the USMC.

– but usually only other engineers, and only those from the same discipline, tend to get the jokes! But the standard one about the micro UAV is that if it is 'micro' then it has to be unmanned – you can't have both.

DARPA and its predecessor ARPA, the people who brought you the Internet, have been involved with unmanned air vehicles for some 20 years, although because most of them have been secret no one would know. These include projects such as Amber (an early predecessor of today's Predator) and the Boeing Condor (a propeller-driven, all-composite, high-endurance UAV). There have been others but they are still in the Black world of top security.

But what is the micro UAV, what is it for and what are some of the problems associated with?

At a recent briefing, a diagram was produced which laid out the performance objective. What was on the slide was a picture of a humming bird! The soldier of the future is not going to be some kind of superhero with the power to talk to the animals: he will have his own mechanical bird which will provide him with pictures, sound and even smells of what is inside a building or bunker.

The size that DARPA is currently aiming at is 6 in, and 'that number is no accident. That number came from a consideration of size and scale and speed that relates to where nature changes the way she operates in terms of the physics of flight control, the physics of aerodynamics. Below that scale, as the birds and insects figured out a long time ago, the game is played very differently. We understand a lot about how nature does it. We have never tried to mechanize flight at this scale before and this program concept is what that's all about.'

The idea of the micro UAV was prompted by efforts at the Lincoln Laboratory to develop a very

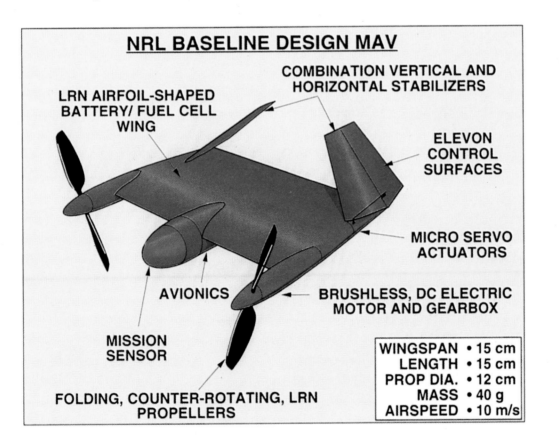

Naval research labs. MITE Micro UAV.

small surveillance platform. What makes this a practical proposition is that the sensors, cameras, microphones etc. to be carried by these types of vehicle are technologically within reach.

Although initially the micro UAV's role was viewed as part of a conventional battlefield, it did not take long to realize that maybe it could help with an increasingly common and deadly environment for the soldier – the urban battlefield of Third World and peace-keeping conflicts. A typical mission might be to check out a house for a sniper or detecting the location of booby-traps by sniffing for explosives. But DARPA and the military would be the first to admit that they are open-minded about the capabilities of such a vehicle and it will only be after they have tried it

out in exercises or in conflicts that they will truly know its uses.

The released configurations of what DARPA-funded projects might look like are fairly conventional. Two have propellers, while one uses a miniature jet that blows the exhaust over its wings. To make the concept smaller than 6 in may require something that looks and behaves more like a dragonfly. For now, the component technologies that would enable the 6 in capability still have major problems, not least being the engine and its power. Electric engines can be made small enough, but even running on a lithium battery they cannot fly for long. A bio-electric motor might be the answer, or some means of the vehicle recharging its power source by sunlight or converting organic

SAM Buster.
McDonnell Douglas
F-4G Wild Weasel –
an invaluable asset
during Desert Storm.

material into gas. Ideas abound, but practical solutions are needed!

The structure of the micro UAV is important. Because of the very small size and weight, the component parts of the sensors and engine will have to form part of the body of the craft. DARPA is talking about a mechanism that approaches an almost organic integration.

Communications, of course, is one of the more rapidly advancing technologies and in terms of line-of-sight communications it can probably shrink the system to do this job. How one then applies that capability to navigate the vehicle and achieve flight control is still a bit of a mystery. GPS is not accurate enough for navigating the rooms of a house and we still do not know how much computer 'smarts', in the form of artificial intelligence, it is possible to place in such a small machine. As is often the case, the TV series *The X-Files* is ahead of the designers. 'The War of the Corprages' episode explored the possibility of alien robots designed to look like cockroaches and fuelled by dung.

The real-world sensors seem to be better in hand. A lot of work at DARPA is going into small sensors, everything from imagery to acoustics, even to biochemical sampling, all on a single microchip.

Communications has to fit in with all these and, of course, they have to be designed to operate in the field. How to keep it from running into somebody and hurting them? How to keep it survivable even in the rucksack? All these very practical matters have to be dealt with. Having a vehicle like this that requires a platoon to launch it makes no sense at all, so whatever is done, it has got to be simple and easy to use – and probably usable by a single soldier.

When, or will, this ever come to pass? The truth, as they say in the *X-Files*, is out there!

'Kelly' Johnson proving that Area-51 does exist!

GOODBYE BOMBER, HELLO AREA-51

The Arab–Israel Yom Kippur War of 1973 was a major shock not only to the Israelis, who came very close to losing, but also to the US military who saw dozens of their best-designed fighters fall victim to a new generation of Soviet-designed air-defence system in a matter of days. And even when flown by the pilots of the Israeli Air Force, arguably the best in the world, these sophisticated aircraft were sustaining crippling losses to the mobile SA-6 'three fingers of death' (Gainful) and the tank-mounted, quadruple cannons of the ZSU-23-4. A number of projects were initiated, but one that was already under way in secret was the use of unmanned aircraft to destroy these deadly SAMs, under the code-name of Have Lemon. The company involved was none other than Teledyne Ryan, and the air vehicle, the classic Firebee with a new designation, the BGM-34A. The airframes, including models which had already seen extensive use in Vietnam, were modified to carry bombs and missiles under the wings and a football-shaped antenna was placed on top of the tail. This last device was the data-link for a TV camera which was situated in the nose of the aircraft. Via this the pilot, safe on the ground or in the launch aircraft, could select the target to receive his weapon.

Under the auspices of the USAF's 6514 Test Squadron, the first full test of the destruction of a SAM site took place on the 14 December 1971. Gene Juberg, who headed the Teledyne Ryan team, describes what happened:

In the nose was a TV camera equipped with a zoom lens, which in real time transmitted an image of the terrain ahead to the screen in the remote-control van. On the drone wing was an AGM-65 Maverick electro-optical seeking missile also capable of telemetering back to control the actual video of the seeker head it had locked on the target. The remote-control operator on the ground was able to see the target on his TV screen about five miles out without using the zoom capability. At about 2.5 miles out, the missile locked on the target and seconds later it was fired under its own power, hitting the target squarely in the centre about nine seconds after firing. It was a historic

A Firebee bomber unleashes a Maverick missile.

first-missile launching from an RPV to score a direct hit. Seven weeks later, in February 1972, an air-launched BQM-34A itself became a launch platform, this time for the 'Stubby Hobo' missile. As an electro-optical glide bomb with an autopilot which drives the vaned control surfaces to give it guidance, the Hobo hit the target squarely.

A simple TV camera was effective at finding small mobile and well-camouflaged SAM sites only under the best weather conditions, so the next step was to give the Firebee an all-weather capability. The BGM-34B had its nose section extended to contain a day or night infrared camera and laser designator designed by Philco-Ford. This system was tested in 1973 and 1974 and proved to be capable of launching and guiding the new generation of laser-guided bombs and missiles coming into use in South-East Asia. But the USAF needed convincing that the system would work not just in the clear weather of California or Utah but in cloud-filled Europe as well. Under the code-name Cornet Thor, six demonstration flights were secretly conducted at a test range in West Germany. All of the objectives were successfully attained.

But resistance within the USAF was strong against the unmanned option, even when it freed up manned aircraft. Such was the case with specially designed jamming and chaff-laying Firebees which proved highly capable in tests but which were never allowed to show their worth operationally.

New Firebee contracts were cancelled but the money saved was only enough to buy spare parts for tactical aircraft. With minimal funding, Teledyne Ryan produced a multimission aircraft that was modular and could be switched from strike missions to reconnaissance or electronic warfare by bolting on separate nose sections or tail units. This was the BGM-34C and it would prove be the most capable Firebee model. However, with the withdrawal from a real shooting war in Vietnam, the unmanned star began to wane. By 1976 the unmanned units, part of Strategic Air Command (SAC), the bomber people, were handed over to Tactical Air Command (TAC), the fighter-bomber people. TAC had little understanding or sympathy for the Firebees and had the priority of rebuilding their stock of sadly depleted tactical fighters. The inevitable happened in 1979: the units were stood down and over 60 Firebees were placed in storage.

Missiles, such as HARM (High-speed Anti

The mock-up of the stealthy General Dynamics/Lockheed A-12 strike/attack aircraft designed to replace the F-111. Although cancelled in 1994, the technology may have been used in a classified unmanned combat aerial vehicle (UCAV) programme. (Lockheed)

What the F-24 Delta
might look like.

Radiation Missile), were introduced to destroy SAM sites and more and more money was spent on the seesaw war of jamming and spoofing equipment. The Cruise missile, essentially a miniature aircraft which used a new generation of computers to navigate and find a fixed target, was initially tasked with nuclear strike, but it was eventually found to be just as capable of delivering conventional weapons. The only thing that bothered the military was that, with it costing

Uninhabited Combat Air Vehicle (UCAV). They range from the relatively mundane, converted F-16s for the Air Force and F-18s for the Navy, to the exotic hypersonic weapons delivery system. As yet they are all unfunded design concepts.

There are two schools of thought about how to design the UCAV: one is essentially evolutionary – design a manned fighter but leave out the cockpit – and the other is revolutionary – design it more like a reusable missile. Whereas the evolutionary

F-117As at the ultra-secret US base at Tonopah, within Area-51, in the Nevada Desert.

around a million dollars apiece, they wanted it to drop its bomb and return to carry out another mission.

UCAVs – The Official Position

There are many plans in the US aerospace community regarding the development of an

approach fulfils the mission requirements, the resulting aircraft does relatively little to reduce the cost of ownership. The reusable missile concept, however, is claimed to produce a saving of between 60 and 90 per cent of the cost of the manned equivalent.

Whereas an aircraft is designed to be flown and maintained on an almost daily basis, a missile will be manufactured and then placed in extended storage until the time comes when it is ready for use. Most manned aircraft flights take place purely for the purpose of training; with the revolutionary UCAV there is no practical difference between flying the simulator and an actual flight, therefore the cost of ownership can be considerably reduced.

stealth design that flies upside down in stealth configuration – which is not practical with a manned plane.

A new generation of low weight/high kill weapons weighing in at less than 20 per cent the weight of normal weapons are planned for these vehicles. These will be guided by a third generation low-cost GPS system and use either a warhead of intermetalic incendiary or flechette design.

Some of the configuration designs look not

The physical design highlights of the UCAV are numerous. It will be capable of manoeuvring at more than 20 times the force of gravity, it is only 40 per cent of the size of the manned equivalent and it has a considerably reduced radar cross section. The UCAV may also be a one-sided

dissimilar to the DarkStar recce UCAV, the cancelled A-12 AvengerII Strike aircraft design and a hypersonic wave-rider design. A 'flying saucer' configuration included in a recent briefing may just be for fun but who knows?

The major technological breakthrough required

With its strange shape
and night-time flying
antics the F-24 Delta
might account for some
UFO sightings.

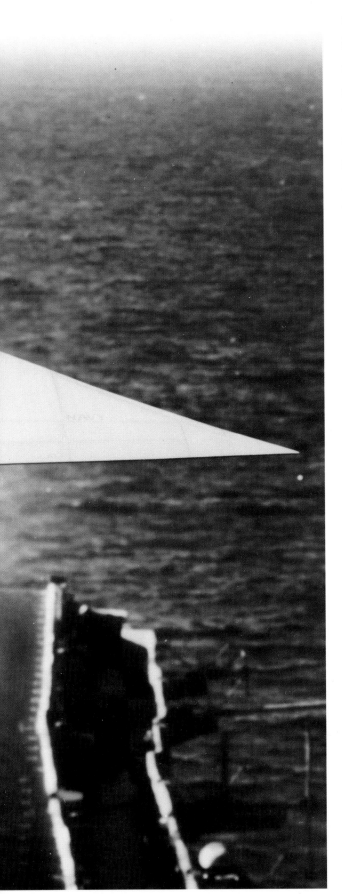

to give this type of aeroplane an operational reality is the capability of beaming the data concerning target imagery back accurately and in a timely manner not just to one or even half a dozen UCAVs but to literally hundreds of these machines. The presentation of this data will benefit from the work already done with simulators and even arcade games. Virtual reality helmets may become *de rigueur* while many of the non-critical/non-lethal functions will be handled automatically by the autonomous computer systems

Many of the above technologies are either on the verge of becoming useful or are maturing quickly.

THE UNOFFICIAL VERSION

There is a massive and unexplainable gap in the capability of the USAF. It is in the area of what is officially called lethal SEAD (Suppression of Enemy Air Defences) but might also be called 'SAM-busting'. It was the destruction of enemy SAMs in Kuwait and Iraq that was vital to the massive air assault in Desert Storm. The widespread export of highly capable Russian SAM designs has led many people to express disbelief at the replacement of the F-4G Wild Weasel with the considerably less capable F-16 Block 50/52. Added to which is the retirement of the only USAF radar jammer, the EF-111A Grey Ghost, in favour of support by US Navy EA-6B Prowlers.

It is this writer's belief that a UCAV for SEAD is currently being tested and/or is operational within the secure site known as Area-51.

THE A-12 MYSTERY AND THE F-24 DELTA

The most likely configuration of the F-24 is that of a flying wing delta, the aerodynamics of which are

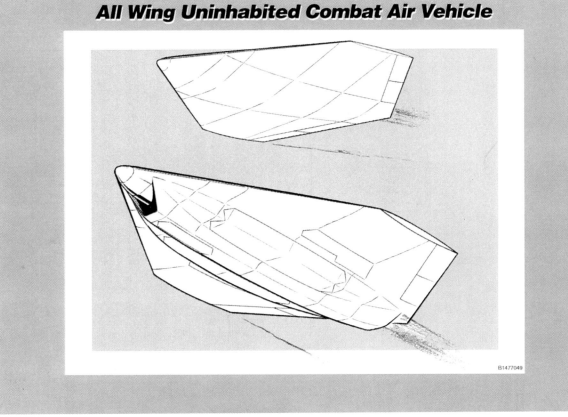

LOCKHEED MARTIN

All Wing Uninhabited Combat Air Vehicle

B1477049

The upside down plane. It turns its stealthy side to the enemy. Pilots may not like flying upside down.

derived from the cancelled General Dynamics (now part of Lockheed Martin)/McDonnell Douglas A-12 AvengerII. This was a subsonic highly stealthy strike aircraft aimed at replacing both the US Navy A-6 Intruders and the USAF F-111s. The A-12 was cancelled in 1991 allegedly because of cost over-runs and the reduction in tension caused by the end of the Cold War and the break-up of the Soviet Union. Although at least $2 billion, and perhaps as much as $4 billion, was spent on the A-12, little hardware has been seen for the money.

With such an exotic aerodynamic design as the A-12, it would be usual for a half-scale flying version to be used for testing the flight characteristics. I believe that this vehicle was produced and flown by the McDonnell Douglas 'Phantom Works' (a 'Skunk Works' type organization) who were also responsible for the

X-36. Flight testing of this unmanned mini A-12 apparently demonstrated an amazing capability in the area of stealth, speed and endurance. It is believed that in 1990, McDonnell Douglas, with its Wild Weasel experience, proposed to the USAF a relatively low cost programme (similar to the X-36) to explore an unmanned replacement for the elderly F-4G. A few million dollars were found to continue the development. The SAM busting experiences of Desert Storm in 1991 increased the flow of money and more extensive secret facilities were made available. With the movement of the F-117 Stealth fighters from Tonopah to Holloman in June 1992, the small, mostly contractor manned, UCAV unit moved in to Tonopah – the most secure air base in the world. Additional money was siphoned from the F-117 budget and the development testing began in earnest.

Opposite page
Carrier based UCAV would be a potent weapon.

This UCAV, which we will refer to as the F-24 Delta, is approximately 25 feet in span and powered by a single, non-after burning General Electric F-404 of 10,600 lbs thrust. It has a relatively small internal centre-line weapons bay.

This aircraft has an operational radius of approximately 600–700 miles so a considerable amount of internal fuel is required; the flying wing design provides the volume for such needs. The long range aspect of the aircraft is required to support deep strike missions, such as during Desert Storm, without the need to refuel in air. The endurance needs to be enough to ensure that the UCAV F-24 can be first into the target area and last out. A typical mission profile might be as follows:

Operating from a secure section of military

base the UCAVs take off as soon as it is dark.

Once the super stealthy F-24s are in a 'SAM rich' zone, a strike package, made up of unmanned decoys, is launched.

As a result, the SAM sites turn on their radars.

The F-24 UCAVs move in close for the kill while exchanging secure messages as to their chosen target with each other and the virtual pilot, located either on the ground or in a command aircraft such as an AWACS.

Passive electro-optical sensors confirm the target, the virtual pilot signs off on the weapons release and a small, maybe 100 lb, laser guided bomb destroys the target. Ten or twelve of such weapons could be carried internally, giving considerable combat persistence

Once the SAM sites realize that they are being

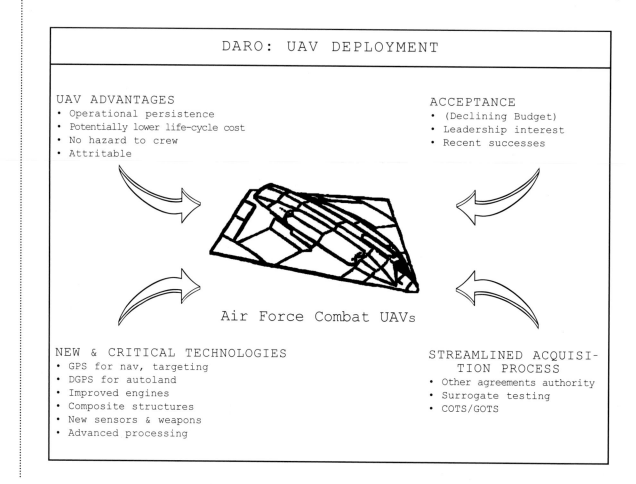

DARO: UAV DEPLOYMENT

UAV ADVANTAGES
• Operational persistence
• Potentially lower life-cycle cost
• No hazard to crew
• Attritable

ACCEPTANCE
• (Declining Budget)
• Leadership interest
• Recent successes

Air Force Combat UAVs

NEW & CRITICAL TECHNOLOGIES
• GPS for nav, targeting
• DGPS for autoland
• Improved engines
• Composite structures
• New sensors & weapons
• Advanced processing

STREAMLINED ACQUISI-
    TION PROCESS
• Other agreements authority
• Surrogate testing
• COTS/GOTS

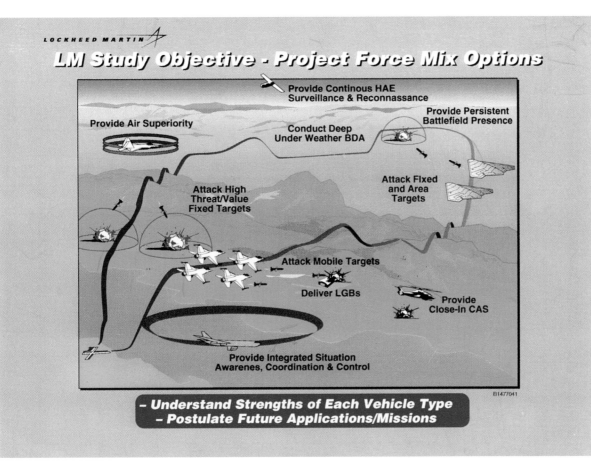

targeted, they are likely to shut down, and move if they are mobile, thus hoping to escape the notice of their invisible nemesis. In this event, using its electro-optical sensors in conjunction with information from systems such as J-STARS, the F-24 can autonomously hunt for likely SAM sites, sending back imagery to the virtual pilot only when it thinks it has a likely target.

It is interesting to note that the USAF in a recent interview said that UCAVs could be available to field by 2007 and that the Israelis are talking about having UCAVs within the next generation. With such confident statements being made, much of the initial work must have already been done!

The original A-12 was also due to have an undisclosed air-to-air capability so these aircraft, although probably subsonic, could be used to test out tactics and technologies that might be used in super-cruise unmanned fighters. Indeed Lockheed Martin are openly discussing the possibility of pilots in their new F-22 Raptor superfighter, controlling three or four unmanned UCAVs. These would fly 50–100 miles in advance of manned aircraft and perform the initial missile exchange, leaving the manned aircraft to mop up the remnants of the enemy.

There is rumoured to be a British connection with the UCAV but typical British secrecy means that this cannot be confirmed.

For those who ask why this project is being kept so secret, the answer may lie in the area of arms reduction treaties. It appears that a UCAV may be classified as a cruise missile and therefore be subject to verifications and limits, or it may mean re-negotiating treaties. Much better to keep it secret.

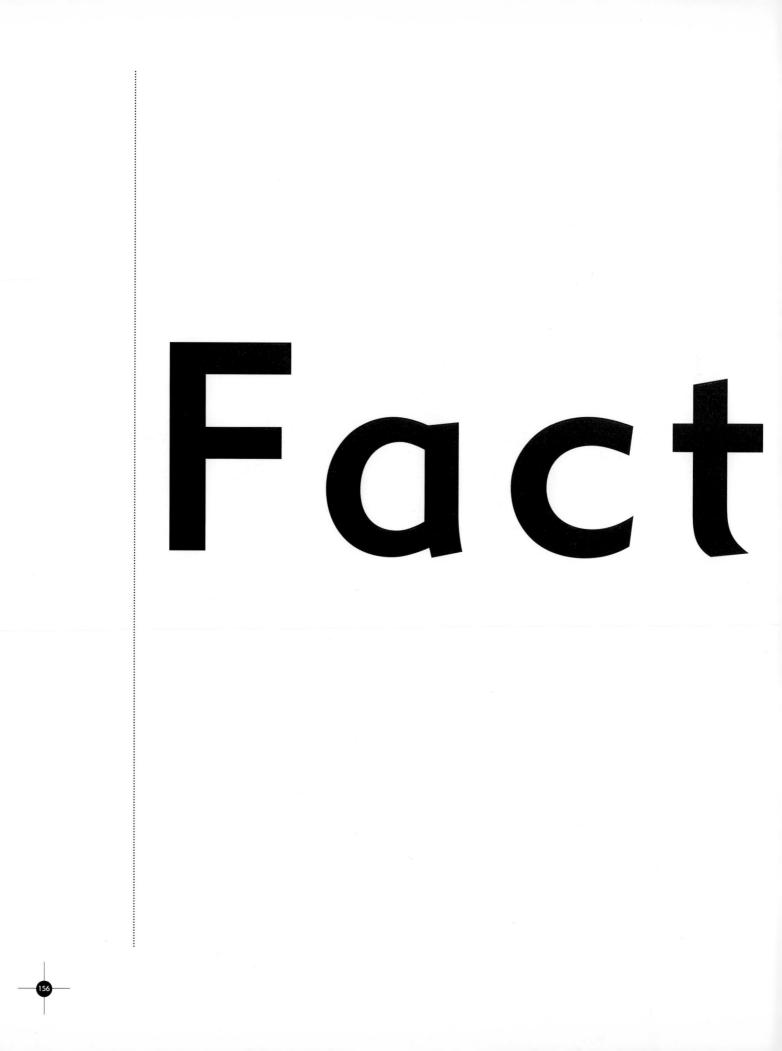

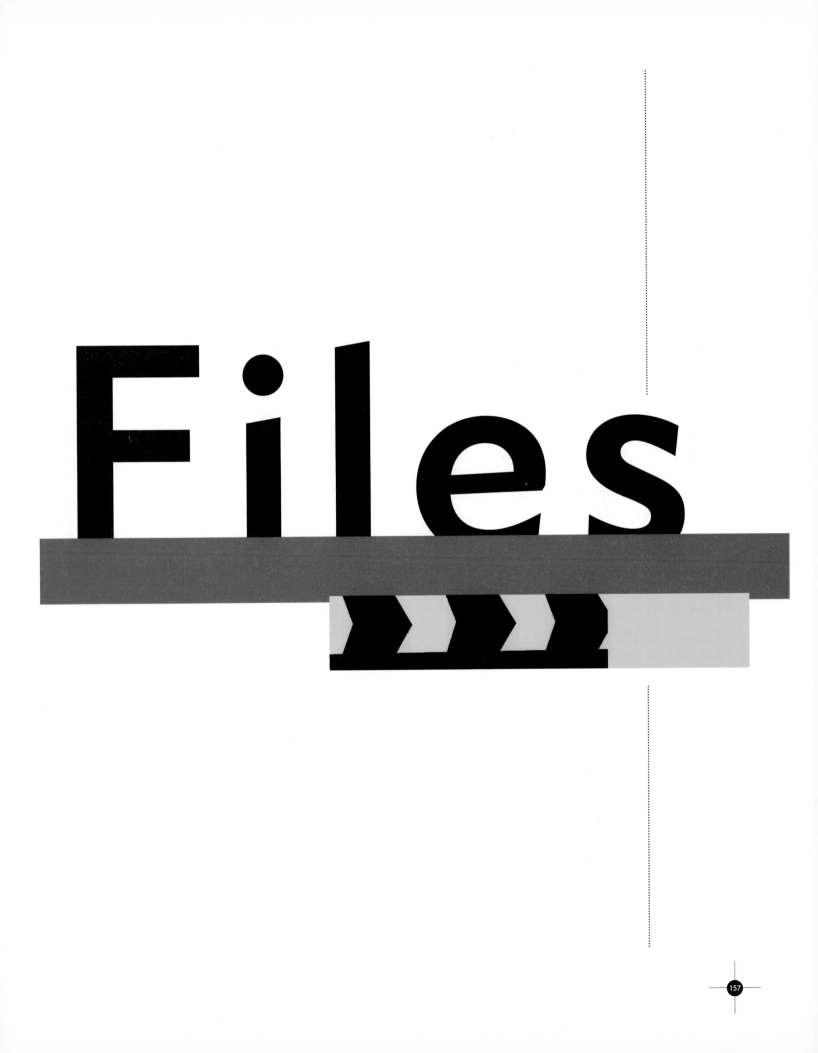

Files

THE BRAVE NEW WORLD

Just in case some readers may find aspects of this book a mite difficult to believe, the following selected passages are included, from a document entitled: *New World Vistas Air and Space Power for the 21st Century.* This is a forecast by the US Air Force Scientific Advisory Panel headed up by Dr Gene H. McCall who, along with some of the best brains available, seeks to identify the scientific development which will result in the USAF gaining the high ground for the decades and century to come. There follows selected sections. The full text of the summary volume is available on the World Wide Web at: http://www.fie.com/fedix/vista.html

New World Vistas Air and Space Power for the 21st Century

This report is a forecast of a potential future for the Air Force. This forecast does not necessarily imply future officially sanctioned programs, planning or policy.

The Future Force

There will be a mix of inhabited and uninhabited aircraft. We use the term 'uninhabited' rather than 'unpiloted' or 'unmanned' to distinguish the aircraft enabled by the new technologies from those now in operation or planned. The 'unmanned' aircraft of the present have particular advantages such as cost or endurance, but they are either cruise missiles or reconnaissance vehicles. The 'uninhabited' combat aircraft

(UCAV) are new, high performance aircraft that are more effective for particular missions than are their inhabited counterparts. The UCAV is enabled by information technologies, but it enables the use of aircraft and weapon technologies that cannot be used in an aircraft that contains a human. There will be missions during the next three decades that will benefit from having a human present, but for many missions the uninhabited aircraft will provide capabilities far superior to those of its inhabited cousins. For example, shape and function will not be constrained by a cockpit, a human body, or an ejection seat. We believe that the design freedom generated will allow a reduction in radar cross section by at least 12 dB in the frequency bands currently addressed, compared to existing aircraft. A 12 dB reduction in aircraft cross section will reduce the effective range of enemy radar by a factor of two and area coverage by a factor of four. At this point we reach the limit of passive radar cross section reduction, and active methods must be developed. Also, reduction of infrared emissions is an important area where substantial improvements can be made. Other advantages of the UCAV will be described later. There is the possibility of extending UCAV performance into the hypersonic range to enable strikes from the CONUS on high value targets in minutes.

Large and small aircraft will project weapons. At present we think of large aircraft as bombers, tankers, surveillance aircraft, or air launched cruise missile (ALCM) launch platforms. In the future large aircraft will be the first to carry directed energy weapons, and their entry into combat as formidable tactical weapons will cause a discontinuous change in aerospace warfare. Eventually, after establishing their value aboard aircraft, directed energy weapons will move into space. Small UCAVs can be carried aboard and launched from large aircraft in order to provide intercontinental standoff capability.

Explosive weapons will be substantially more accurate than those of today, and explosive effectiveness per unit mass will be higher by at least a factor of ten than those of today. As a result, a sortie of the future can be ten times more effective than one of today. Weapon types will range from inexpensive enhanced accuracy weapons without sensors to GPS directed weapons with better than one foot accuracy to microsensor directed microexplosive systems that kill moving targets with grams of explosive.

The trade between munition precision and platform precision will, of course, depend on the survivability of the platform at appropriate release distances and the dependence of cost on munition accuracy. It may be possible to reduce the cost of precision delivery by building reusable, close approach delivery platforms that have precision positioning and sensing systems, reproducible weapon release, and wind measuring equipment onboard. Munitions can be built with low drag coefficients. Significant cost reduction will result from the reuse of sensors and processors. The munition can either have no guidance or can have simple inertial or GPS guidance and low precision controls. This option favors the low observable UCAV for attack of mobile and protected targets.

This low resolution snapshot of the Force was intended to give the reader an idea of the extensive enhancement and integration of capabilities that will be possible in future decades. We hope that the applications of the new technologies are so profound that they are obvious and compelling, and we hope that they stimulate the reader to create personally pleasing combinations of capabilities. For example, improved stealth provides higher effectiveness against both aircraft and SAMs in establishing air superiority. Improved aircraft performance, say through UCAVs, will increase survivability in high threat areas. Together, stealth and performance will reduce the reliance on electronic countermeasures with an accompanying reduction in cost and system volatility, and when directed by offboard information and passive sensors, they have the surprise value of a silent force. Large airlifters with point of use delivery capability can provide the military equivalent of 'just in time' supply from CONUS, if necessary, with cost reductions and efficiency increases that are as large as those realized by commercial industries. Accompanied by airlifters carrying UCAVs and directed energy weapons for self defense, the airlifter fleet will become a survivable offensive weapon system in high threat areas. Distributed space systems can revisit areas of interest at rates not now possible. Distributed space sensors can operate cooperatively with staring sensors aboard Uninhabited Reconnaissance Air Vehicles (URAVs), which continuously monitor important targets, to optimize the collection and use of intelligence information.

Standoff Systems

The systems described in Sec. 2.1 are non-intrusive. At the next level of involvement other possibilities arise. If it is possible to position vehicles within 200–300 nm of a region of interest, high resolution staring sensors and SARs can be carried on URAVs that loiter at 50,000 – 100,000 feet. Figure II-2 shows range to the horizon from a given altitude.

Continuous monitoring at a resolution of one meter or less is possible. URAVs can work cooperatively with satellite constellations by projecting high power RF beams over the area of interest. The satellites receive reflected signals from targets near the earth to form a distributed bistatic synthetic aperture radar system. Clutter rejection is improved because of the varying reflection angles to different satellites. Moving and fixed targets can be detected with high resolution as the result of the long baseline between satellites. This arrangement limits the number of expensive spaceborne transmitters by restricting coverage to a region of interest. We have added:

5. Continuous Multispectral and SAR observation at 1 meter resolution 6. Continuous bistatic detection and tracking of fixed and moving targets over a limited area.

Overhead URAV Systems

Further improvement in resolution can be obtained in situations where overflight of enemy territory is authorized. Low observable URAVs can carry staring and scanning sensors which produce multispectral and SAR images and LIDAR returns at few centimeter resolution. The URAVs can deploy low altitude or ground based chemical sensors for accurate discrimination of Chemical & Biological (CB) agents and the effluents from Nuclear, Chemical and Biological (NCB) manufacturing plants. These sensors can be interrogated by driving readout with an RF or optical signal from a satellite or a URAV. The remotely read sensor will have reduced size, weight, power, and vulnerability. Now, the system consists of:

7. Continuous multispectral and SAR observation at 1 centimeter resolution 8. Contact sensors for NCB detection.

Unattended Ground Sensors

We mentioned the integration of ground sensors into the Global Awareness network as NCB detectors, but a few specific observations should be made. Unattended ground sensors are at present difficult to deploy and to monitor. Deployment by manned intrusion, air or ground, is the norm.[5] It is not clear that deployment and operation are Air Force missions. Technologies now under development and the need for detailed awareness in specific areas of the world can change the situation completely. In addition to NCB detectors, ground sensors are natural candidates to monitor the local weather. Weather monitoring from space is possible, but ground monitoring can be more accurate, more continuous, and far less expensive.

Ground sensors can be deployed by miniature UAVs carried aboard larger UAVs. Microsensor development is proceeding, and, as noted, novel readout methods which have a low probability of intercept (LPI) have been proposed. The Air Force should investigate the advantages of ground sensors for local monitoring before committing to more expensive space and airborne sensors.

After a decade from now, URAV deployment is likely to be the method of choice, although there is a long term possibility for shifting the balance of continuous surveillance completely back to space. It has been proposed that very large, lightweight structures can be deployed in space to create optics and antennas having dimensions of kilometers.[6] It is the product of power and aperture that determines signal-to-noise, all other factors being equal. The URAV and space options are attractive as replacements for AWACS and Joint STARS. Both the AWACS and the Joint STARS use much of their volume for crew and displays, and loiter time is restricted by fuel consumption and crew limits. The systems of the early 21st century should use high speed processors which will exceed current performance by a factor of 10,000 for AWACS and 1000 for Joint STARS. Processor volume should be no more than $1m^3$. Communication rates of 100 MHz to satellites will be practical almost immediately, and lasercom will appear in a decade. Multiple URAVs can detect and process signals coherently to provide large increases in resolution, and loiter times of tens of hours without refueling are possible.

5.1 AIRCRAFT AND SYSTEMS FOR POWER PROJECTION.

We explored the enhancement of existing aircraft and weapon systems during the study on Life Extension and Mission Enhancement for Air Force Aircraft.[27] The study identified avionics and training as the highest leverage technologies for improving the capabilities of the existing fleet. Those suggestions are appropriate for integrating the current fleet into the capabilities described in this report. Here we describe the justification of the Uninhabited Combat Air Vehicle (UCAV).

UCAV

An effective UCAV will be enabled in the next century as the result of the simultaneous optimization of information flow, aircraft performance, and mission effectiveness. The UCAV will not completely replace the inhabited aircraft for decades, if ever, but the presence, or absence, of a pilot is now a design trade that can be made in a logical way.

It is the improvements in sensors, processors, and information networks which make the UCAV possible. Information will increasingly be derived from sensors outside the air vehicle itself. Current concepts call for transmitting information derived from many sources over a satellite or ground-based link to the pilot of a high performance combat aircraft. The amount of information which can be injected into the cockpit is enormous.

Discussion of pilot overload is common. More displays are needed in an already crowded cockpit, and more attention is demanded from an already overworked pilot. The question which must be asked, then, is whether it is more efficient to bring the pilot to the information rather than to bring the information to the pilot. The usual UAV issues, such as survivability, are secondary if performance is not compromised. When one considers the volume of information which will be necessary to conduct precision, high intensity operations of the future, it is possible that the most economical use of communication resources will be to transmit low bandwidth control, or control correction, information to the aircraft rather than to transmit mission information. The decision to use UCAVs will, of course, depend on the theater environment which has many variables such as the density of enemy jammers.

Information gathered from many sources, included from the UCAV, itself, will be brought to the Execution Control Center, which is located in the US, over high speed, massively redundant fiber and satellite communication routes. A permanent environmentally controlled installation will permit extensive use of state-of-the-art commercial equipment. Vehicle cost and weight will be reduced because of the absence of displays, pilot life support equipment, and manual controls. Volume, area, and weight of displays, processors, and controls in the Control Center can be large. Well rested mission specialists will be available to provide support for one or more UCAVs, and a cadre of expert, possibly civilian, maintenance technicians will also be available. The number of support personnel in the theater will be reduced, and it will not be necessary to transport a large number of shelters, workstations, and environmental control units. Extremely low observability of the UCAV will result in the reduction of standoff distance at the weapon release point and will, in turn, reduce weapon sensor, guidance, and propulsion costs.

Control technologies for UCAVs are not mature. The interaction between airframe and pilot will be cooperative and variable to a much greater extent than in existing aircraft. The pilot(s) will provide general direction in realtime when this is necessary. Control functions will be enabled by software agents transmitted from the Control Center. Agents will permit function changes such as from ground attack to air defense during a mission. Unplanned maneuvers can be generated in realtime.

UCAV survivability can be increased by increasing maneuverability beyond that which can be tolerated by a human pilot. Acceleration limits for inhabited aircraft are, typically, +9 g or 10 g and -3 g. A UCAV can be designed symmetrically to accelerate in any direction immediately. Anti-aircraft missiles are usually designed with a factor of three margin in lateral acceleration over that of the target aircraft, although a few missiles have acceleration capability as high as 80 g. A UCAV with a ±10 g capability could outfly many missiles, and an acceleration capability of ±20 g will make the UCAV superior to nearly all missiles.

Removal of the pilot from the aircraft also

makes possible more options for signature suppression. Inhabited aircraft have limited options of shape and cross sectional area which limit the options for minimizing drag and radar cross section. Maneuvers and flight attitudes not appropriate for inhabited aircraft can also be executed to reduce the cross section presented to an adversary. The UCAV will also provide design flexibility for active stealth systems when they are developed.

The Air Force should pursue the design of a UCAV. It appears logical to begin with cruise missile parameters such as those of the Advanced Cruise Missile and then to increase capabilities by scaling. The inverse procedure of scaling down from an inhabited aircraft, say the F-22, may lead to higher cost and cross section. Operational concepts should be developed, and new weapon options should be pursued. Novel methods to optimize the interaction of remote pilots with a UCAV should be explored through simulation. Control and communication methods should be developed. The point to be made here is that the UCAV is a unique aircraft, and it should be designed as such.

Terrorists in Urban Areas

Terrorist operations are usually characterized by the proximity of noncombatants. Hostage situations are possible. These situations are treated at present by special teams using appropriate weapons. Air Force participation is limited to delivery of combat teams and supplies. In the future, however, the development of sublethal weapons deployed from aircraft and URAV sensors will increase Air Force responsibilities in this area. A weapon which can have a very large impact on urban warfare and hostage situations is discussed in the classified section of the report.

Short Dwell Targets

We define short dwell targets as those that are vulnerable for a time short enough that their vulnerability is determined by the exposure time rather than by characteristics of an attacking weapon. Mobile missile launchers are an example. Launchers can be concealed, camouflaged, or protected by a structure until ready for use. After use they can be moved rapidly to a protected, or concealed, position. It is the protection of the target which distinguishes it from a mobile target.

Attack on short dwell targets is enabled by two factors – identification and weapon delivery. The Global Awareness system will detect and identify a target. If there is a URAV staring at the area of interest,[31] the Global Awareness system will deliver target coordinates to an accuracy of one meter or better, and the Dynamic Planning and Execution Control system can target a coordinate-seeking weapon in seconds. Detection by satellite constellation to an accuracy of 2–3 meters is adequate for the deployment of weapons having warheads of 50–100 kg. Targets such as Multiple Launch Rocket Systems (MLRS) and Transporter Erector Launchers (TEL) for theater ballistic missiles will be particularly vulnerable to this weapon system if weapon delivery times are short enough. If observation is by a URAV, an accuracy of 30 cm or less can be obtained, and warheads as small as 0.1–1 kg can be used. These weapons can be carried aboard the URAV. SIGINT detection by a distributed satellite constellation followed by coordinate transfer to a weapon will be extraordinarily effective against SAM sites and other facilities which radiate infrequently.

The best known short dwell target is the theater ballistic missile (TBM).

The UCAV can be designed as a hypersonic weapon delivery platform. Reusable UCAVs which deliver unguided or coordinate guided weapons may be cost effective when compared to individual missile costs of $1M. For the UCAV, air breathing propulsion or a combination of rocket and air breathing propulsion may be the system of choice. Design and construction of a hypersonic aircraft at 4–5 km/s, Mach 12–15, will be complex and will require new airframe and propulsion technologies. Flight altitudes will range from 25–45 km (85,000–150,000 feet). A hypersonic UCAV will, undoubtedly, be far less expensive than a manned vehicle, and performance will be superior. For example, higher skin temperatures can be tolerated. The vehicle will transition from subsonic to supersonic to hypersonic flight as altitude increases and will transition back to lower speed and altitudes near the target. Velocity transition will obviate the need for a new class of weapons for hypersonic release.[33]

Commercial Technology

Entertainment companies are developing at breakneck speeds new ways for humans to interact with machines. The intensity of the battle among companies is indicated by their being among the most profitable corporations in the world. While companies do not publish their investments in technology development, it is probable that these investments dwarf that of the Department of Defense (DoD). It is certainly true that the best students in computer and information science are vying for positions in entertainment companies.

It may be that no specific products of the entertainment industry will be of use to the Air Force. However, the thrust of entertainment technology is to convey a sense of 'being there' to an audience or to a group of participants. Successful development of such a technology would qualify it as revolutionary. The impact on teleconferencing, collaboration at a distance, flight simulation, UCAV operation, and many other applications would be enormous. We urge the Air Force to establish continuing contact as closely as possible with entertainment organizations.

Primary Technologies

At this point the reader has probably concluded that the technological Air Force of the 21st century may be effective, but that it will certainly be incredibly complicated and unaffordable. If the capabilities described earlier were developed as the sum of many systems, both statements would be true. In fact, if the overall capability of the Force were merely the sum of capabilities of individual systems, a modern Air Force would be unaffordable. We have emphasized that the strength of New World Vistas technologies lies in their integration. To demonstrate this assertion we will identify the individual technologies necessary for achieving the result we propose. A detailed list and recommended actions will be given in Chapter III. Technologies marked with a (R) will generate revolutionary capabilities. Technologies marked with an asterisk (*) will be pursued in both commercial and military forms. It is currently not clear whether the Air Force decision should be to develop or to buy. They are duplicated on the list.

Technologies to be developed:

* (R)UCAV structures and engines – including hypersonic operation

* Remote control technologies

* Nonlinear optic compensation

* (R)Active and IR stealth

* Hyperspectral sensing and target identification at low spatial resolution

* (R)Human-Machine interactions *

* Micro-electro-mechanical systems for sensing and manipulating *

* Uninhabited Combat Aerial Vehicles (UCAV).

As this technology is developed it will offer potential for significantly more capable weapon systems at lower cost. Such vehicles serendipitously accommodate the probably inexorable trend of American society which are more and more expecting no human losses during US. military operations. The technologies to realize the UCAV include new high efficiency, high supersonic engines; advanced structures; avionics, control systems, and observables; very high altitude/low speed cruise, very small/miniaturized 'micro-air vehicles'; very high dynamic pressure cruise vehicles; intelligent signal and data processing; secure and possibly redundant control data links; control science and applications for mission and vehicle management of a complex, highly coupled system, control criteria to achieve optimal performance based on that used for missile control; and human/machine interface for off board air vehicle control.

HYPERSONIC UAVs

The following is part of a research paper produced as part of the Air Force 2025 discussion document. SHAAFT is an acronym for Supersonic/ Hypersonic Attack Aircraft.

Numerous technological challenges will have to be met before the proposed integrated, multistage weapons system can be built. However, none of these challenges presupposes that a breakthrough in technology is an enabling requirement. The zeroth-stage flying wing is a UAV with a maximum mach number of 3.5. While that is slightly above the mach number for the current high-speed civil transport design, it should not be difficult to solve the problems unique to this application, given that the proposed system would be fielded in the twenty-first century.

The design of the SHAAFT offers the greatest challenges because there exist no vehicles that have flown at sustained hypersonic speeds while powered by an airbreathing system. Furthermore, the aircraft should have global range with a payload of approximately 50,000 pounds. The use of a flying wing to transport the SHAAFT to the one-third point of its global range mission at a mach number of 3.5 greatly simplifies the design of the SHAAFT. Considerable weight savings occur because the flying wing will carry the fuel required for takeoff, acceleration, and flight to the one-third point. The SHAAFT won't need heavy landing gear to support the takeoff weight. Furthermore, it does not need a zero-speed or a low-speed propulsion system. It appears that a dual-mode ramjet/scramjet combustor could be used to accelerate the vehicle from mach 3.5 to its cruise mach number of eight or of 12 and to sustain flight in this speed range. The decision as to whether to limit the vehicle design to mach 8 flight or to extend its capabilities to mach 12 flight is dominated by the propulsion system. Assuming reasonable development of the technologies of hypersonic-airbreathing propulsion systems and their fuels, it is assumed that mach 8 is the upper limit for the use of endothermic hydrocarbon fuels. One will need cryogenic fuels to extend the maximum cruise speed to mach 12. Some of the pros and cons of this problem are presented in the Critical Technology Requirements chapter, tables 5-1 and 5-2. Based on the survivability and on the range of the SHAAFT as a weapons platform for delivering SHMACs and as the initial stages for the SCREMAR, mach 12 flight would probably be preferred. Based on considerations relating to ground operations and support, especially if a recovery base is needed as an intermediate host, the endothermic fuels support a decision to limit the vehicle to a maximum mach number of eight. In any case, a serious trade study (including the

effect on the design of the TAV/orbiter and its payload) should be conducted at the outset of the SHAAFT program.

An aerothermodynamically efficient vehicle having a hypersonic lift-to-drag ratio of five, or better, will be a long, slender body with relatively small leading-edge radii (the nose radius, the cowl radius, and the wing leading-edge radius). Thus, the heating rates in these regions will be relatively high. Controlling the vehicle weight will have a high priority. Therefore, the development of high-strength, lightweight materials and the ability to efficiently use them for the load-carrying structure and for the thermal protection system are high-priority items. Researchers at the National Aeronautics and Space Administration's Ames Research Center (NASA) are developing advanced Diboride Ceramic Matrix Composites (CMC), including Zirconium Dibirode and Hafnium Diboride materials which are reportedly able to withstand repeated exposure to temperatures of

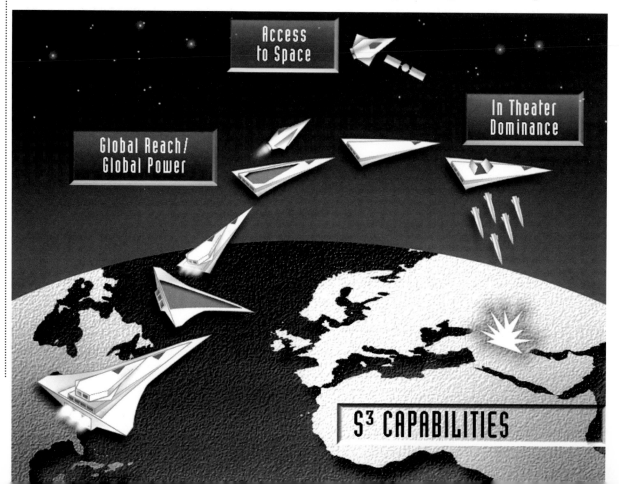

3660 degrees fahrenheit and of 4,130 degrees fahrenheit, respectively. Materials for thermal protection systems developed for Shuttle derivatives, for the NASP, for the X-33, and for the X-34 should be reviewed for use in the proposed weapons system.

Major problems facing the aerothermodynamicist include the determination of boundary-layer transition criteria and the complex viscous/inviscid interaction associated with the multiple shock waves that occur, when the payloads (either the SHMACs or the SCREMAR) are released from the SHAAFT. The problem of developing boundary-layer transition criteria challenged the developers of the first reentry vehicles; it challenged the developers of the NASP; and it will challenge the developers of the SHAAFT. In the end, most likely, a criteria will be selected (with a degree of conservatism appropriate to the acceptable risk) and the design will proceed. The problem of shock/shock interactions associated with two objects flying in close proximity at hypersonic should be solvable. Some work has already been done on the staging of the Sanger.

The decision to limit the SHMAC to a maximum flight mach number of eight was straight forward. Since a variant of the SHMACs will be launched from conventional aircraft, such as the F-22 or the F-15E, simplicity of ground operations, of fuel handling, and of weapons loading at forward bases dictates against cryogenic fuels. By limiting the SHMAC to a maximum mach number of eight, hydrocarbon fuels can be used. Use of hydrocarbon fuels instead of cryogenics greatly simplifies in-theater logistics, ground-support operations, and training requirements for base personnel. However, the SHMAC design must accommodate the transient loads associated with the short-duration overspeed when being launched from the SHAAFT.

Technology developments will be needed in the areas of guidance, navigation, and control (GN&C) and sensors for both the SHAAFT and SHMAC. Large changes in weight and in weight distribution will occur during the flight of the SHAAFT. Control of an aircraft flying at hypersonic speeds over great ranges requires advances in the state of the art. Collection and interpretation of data (threats, targets, political considerations at the brink of war) and decisions as to how to react must be continuously incorporated into the mission plan.

The design of the TAV/orbiter, a.k.a. the SCREMAR, should make use of the large number of access-to-space programs continuing around the world, including international programs, such as, the Japanese HOPE, as well as US programs, such as the X-33, the X-34, and the XCRV (currently under development at NASA). Since the SCREMAR is all rocket powered and operates in a similar manner as the Space Shuttle once separated from the SHAAFT, it should use as much of the current technology incorporated by the Space Shuttle as possible.

The technology programs used to develop the SHAAFT can be transferred directly to the SHMAC and SCREMAR, and vice versa. This is another application of the term integrated weapons system. The development of the S3 concept as a single weapons platform with several similar and fully compatible vehicles will be much easier on the technology demands as well the development costs than attempting to fulfill the same roles with different weapons systems.

BREVEL

ROLE: Tactical surveillance, target acquisition/designation, damage assessment
COUNTRY: Eurodrone GIE (Matra Defence, France, and STN Atlas Elektronik,Germany)

POWER PLANT: 1 x piston engine. Sachs SF 2/350, 22 kW
DIMENSIONS: Span 11.15 ft; length 7.41ft; height 2.99 R
WEIGHTS: Gross 331 lb
PERFORMANCE: Cruising speed 81 kt; max speed 135 kt; ceiling 13,123 ft; mission radius 27–43 nm; endurance over 4 hours

SENSORS: 8-12 pm FLIR (possible options TV/EW/ECM)
DATA LINK: HF (jamming resistant) radio command uplink; real-time imagery data downlink
LAUNCH: Rocket boost from truck-mounted container
GUIDANCE/TRACKING: Pre-programmed remote control
RECOVERY: Parachute and airbag

CUSTOMER: French and German Armies

Brevel (from Bremen and Velizy – its manufacturers' factory and locations) is a small-size, lightweight stealthy UAV being developed under a 1992 six-year contract for service entry in 1997–98. The TUCAN-95 UAV-expoa version, with an endurance of up to 10 hours, is based on Brevet technology and will be ready for operation in 1995.

CANARD ROTOR/WING

ROLE: Reconnaissance/surveillance
COUNTRY: McDonnell Douglas Helicopter Systems, USA

POWER PLANT: 1 x low-bypass turbofan, rated at 707 lb thrust
DIMENSIONS: Span/rotor diameter 14 ft; length 17.25 ft; tail span 9.5 ft; height 5.25 ft
WEIGHTS: Max. payload 200 lb; design max gross 1,785 lb
PERFORMANCE (ESTIMATED): Dash speed more than 375 kt; mission radius 150 nm; mid-mission loiter 3 hours; max range at 10,000 ft 980 nm

SENSORS: Various, according to customer requirements
DATA LINK: Not stated
LAUNCH: Vertical take-off
GUIDANCE/TRACKING: Pre-programmed, GPS navigation
RECOVERY: Vertical landing

CUSTOMER: Adaptable to various US armed forces requirements

The CB/W performs like a rotary-wing aircraft for take-off, hover and landing. Exhaust and bypass gases are ducted to nozzles near the rotor/wing tips to maintain rotation. For fixed-wing flight the rotor/wing is stopped and locked at 120–150 kt (222–278 km/h) forward speed and the gases diverted to provide conventional forward thrust, active controls on the canards and tail plane governing aircraft altitude and direction.

CRECERELLE

ROLE: Tactical reconnaissance and surveillance; target acquisition
COUNTRY: Group SAGEM (SAGEM & SAT), France

POWER PLANT: I x piston engine, rated at 26 hp
DIMENSIONS: Span 10.83 ft; length 9.02ft; height 2.33 ft; payload volume 1.77 ft
WEIGHTS: Empty 100 lb; max. payload 77 lb; max. gross 265 lb
PERFORMANCE: Max. speed 135 kt; loiter speed 65 kt; ceiling 11,000 ft; mission radius 32 nm; endurance over 5 hours

SENSORS: SAT Cyclops 2000 IRLS-, FLIR; EW
DATA LINK: TTL radio command uplink; real-time video down link
LAUNCH: Catapult from trailer-mounted zero length launcher
GUIDANCE/TRACKING: Pre-programmed. RF or GPS navigation (air vehicle position better than 32.8ft CEP)
RECOVERY: Parachute or belly skid landing

CUSTOMER: French Army

Crecerelle (Kestrel) is in operation with the French Army. Each system comprises a mobile ground segment on two 5-ton class military trucks, plus six air vehicles.

CYPHER

ROLE: Close-range battlefield surveillance, mine detection, environmental monitoring
COUNTRY: Sikorsky Aircraft, USA

POWER PLANT: 1 x Alvis AR 801 rotary piston engine, rated at 52 hp
DIMENSIONS: Overall diameter 6.50 ft; rotor diameter 4.00 ft; height 2.00 ft
WEIGHTS: Empty 175 lb; max. payload 45 lb; max. gross 300 lb
PERFORMANCE: Cruising speed over 80 kt; ceiling 5,000 ft; mission radius up to 16 nm beyond FLOT; endurance 3 hours

SENSORS: Daylight TV camera; FLIR; communications relay; EW
DATA LINK: Radio command uplink; real-time imagery/data downlink
LAUNCH: Vertical take-off
GUIDANCE/TRACKING: Remote control of speed, altitude and way point instructions otherwise autonomous; GPS-based INS navigation
RECOVERY: Vertical landing

CUSTOMER: Development continuing for military and commercial applications

Cypher was originally aimed at the row-suspended UAV-Manoeuvre US military requirement, making a tethered first flight in April 1992 and its first free flight in early 1993. Company development flying was continuing in 1994.

D-21

ROLE: Reconnaissance/surveillance
COUNTRY: Lockheed Martin Skunk Works, USA

POWER PLANT: Marquardt RJ-43-MA-3 ramjet
DIMENSIONS: Span 19 ft; length 43 ft; height 6 ft
WEIGHT: 11,200 lb without booster
PERFORMANCE: Speed Mach 3.5+; ceiling 90,000+ ft; range 3,500+ miles (perhaps up to 10,000 miles)

SENSOR: Hycon Optical Camera, wet film
DATA LINK: None
LAUNCHER: Lockheed M-12 Blackbird
GUIDANCE: Pre-programmed, Honeywell INS plus Stellar Navigation
RECOVERY: Non-recoverable except for camera and film pod

CUSTOMER: CIA/USAF/NASA 38

The Lockheed D-21 is an unmanned or 'drone' aircraft designed to carry out high-speed, high-altitude strategic reconnaissance missions over hostile territory. It is a product of the Lockheed 'Skunk Works' program that developed the A-12, YF-12, and SR-71 'Blackbird' manned aircraft in the 1960s.

DR.3/VR3

ROLE: Tactical reconnaissance and surveillance
COUNTRY: Tupolev OKB, Russia

POWER PLANT: 1 x TR-3-117 turbojet, rated at 1,301 lb thrust
DIMENSIONS: Span 7.38 ft; length 6.89 ft (26.44 ft including booster)
WEIGHTS: Max. gross 3,064 lb with film camera; 3,108 lb with TV camera
PERFORMANCE: Max. speed 500 kt; operating altitude 660–3,280 ft; mission radius 38 nm; endurance 13 minutes

SENSORS: PA-1 aerial camera or CHibis-B TV camera
DATA LINK: Video downlink
LAUNCH: Rocket boost from truck-mounted container; possibly also air-launched
GUIDANCE/TRACKING: Pre-programmed
RECOVERY: Parachute descent; three-point landing on retractable landing skids

CUSTOMER: Soviet/Russian Air Force; armed forces of former Warsaw Pact nations; exports to Syria and perhaps also Iraq in 1980s

Developed in the early 1970s and still a standard Russian system (complete system is named *Reys: Voyage*); Czech version designated VR-3. A longer-range version was developed in the late 1970s, named *Strizh* (Martlet); it is thought to have entered limited service in about 1983.

EAGLE EYE

ROLE: Reconnaissance, surveillance, targeting, acquisition (US Government name TiltRotor) UAV System (TRUS)
COUNTRY: Bell Helicopter Textron, USA

POWER PLANT: 1 x Allison 250-C20, heavy fuel (JP-8, F-34 etc)
DIMENSIONS: Overall length 17.90 ft; wing-span 15.20 ft; rotor diameter 9.50 ft
WEIGHTS: Payload 100–300 lb; max. gross weight 2000 lb
PERFORMANCE: Max. speed minus 30 to greater than 200; endurance 8 hours with 100 lb payload; altitude 20,000 ft

SENSORS: JT-UAV EO/IR sensor
DATA LINK: JT-UAV C Band 110 nm radius others
LAUNCH: No launch and recovery equipment required
GUIDANCE/TRACKING: JT-UAV / TAC3 based GCS
RECOVERY: Embedded land based automated launch and recovery

CUSTOMER: US Government, civil, international
First flown in July 1 993, Eagle Eye is a low-cost, all-composite tilt-rotor air vehicle using extensive off-the-shelf helicopter and common hardware parts. Transitions between helicopter and aeroplane modes of flight began in February 1994.

EYE-VIEW

ROLE: Reconnaissance, surveillance, targeting
COUNTRY: IAI Malat, Israel

POWER PLANT: 1 x 25 hp piston
DIMENSIONS: Span approx. 13 ft; length 9.5 ft
WEIGHTS: Payload 30 lb; max. take off 230 lb
PERFORMANCE: Max. speed 100+kt; ceiling 5000+ ft; mission radius 150 nm; max. endurance more than 6 hours

SENSOR: Electro-optical camera or FLIR
GUIDANCE/TRACKING: Innertial
LAUNCH/RECOVERY: Conventional wheeled take-off

CUSTOMER: In development

Also being marketed in the Civil Market as FireBird for Forestry Protection.

EXDRONE

ROLE: EW, reconnaissance or communications relay
COUNTRY: BAI Aerasystems Inc., USA

POWER PLANT: 1 x piston engine, rated at 5.2 hp (optionally 22 hp)
DIMENSIONS: Span 8.00 ft; length 5.25 ft
WEIGHTS: Empty 34 lb; payload (incl fuel) 43 lb; max. gross 77 lb
PERFORMANCE: Max. speed 100 kt; loiter speed 39–65 kt; range 65 nm

SENSORS: Daylight colour TV
DATA LINK: Real-time video down ink, L-band
LAUNCH: Rocket boost or pneumatic launch rail
GUIDANCE/TRACKING: Remote control or GPS auto navigation
RECOVERY: Parachute or skid landing

CUSTOMER: US Navy and Marine Corps (BQM-147A)

Exdrone's name derives from its original purpose – that of an expendable electronic warfare (jamming) UAV. However, in the 1991 Gulf war it became useful for reconnaissance too, with a small TV camera and microwave video transmitter. More are now on order, for reconnaissance, jamming and communications relay. In March 1994 a widebody variant was flown by US Marines. This system utilized a larger 22 hp engine with 250 watt alternator and showed the capability to carry aloft 32 lb of pure payload.

'FIREBEE' BQM-34

ROLE: Aerial Target
COUNTRY: Ryan, USA

ENGINE: Continental J69-T-29 of 1,700 lb thrust
DIMENSIONS: Span 12.11 ft; length 22.11 ft; height 6.7 ft
WEIGHT: 2,062 lb loaded
PERFORMANCE: Maximum speed 550 kt; stalling speed 160 kt; range 600 miles; service ceiling 51,300 ft

The Firebee, originally designated the Q-2, is a high-speed target drone for both surface-to-air and air-to-air missiles. It is used primarily for the testing of newly developed missiles and for the training of fighter-interceptor pilots whose aircraft are armed with missiles.

Capable of being launched from the ground or from an aeroplane in flight, the Firebee is radio-controlled during its mission by an operator on the ground. Upon being hit by a missile and disabled, or upon completing its mission undamaged, the Firebee is lowered safely to earth by a self-contained parachute.

'FIREBEE' AQM-34L

ROLE: Reconnaissance Vehicle
COUNTRY: Teledyne Ryan, USA

ENGINE: Teledyne Continental J-69 of 1,920 lb thrust
DIMENSIONS: Span 13 ft; length 29 ft; height 6.8 ft
WEIGHT: 3,200 lb loaded
PERFORMANCE: Maximum speed 630 kt; cruising speed 450 kt; range 750 miles; service ceiling 50,000 ft; mission altitude 200–500 ft

The AQM-34L reconnaissance drone was developed from the earlier BQM-34A (formerly designated Q-2-C) jet-powered, subsonic target drone first produced in 1960. It is one of a series of remotely piloted vehicles (RPVs) used for combat reconnaissance during the Vietnam War. The AQM-34L was air-launched and controlled from a DC-130 director aircraft and flown on low-level photographic missions over North Vietnam. After a mission, the RPV was directed to a safe recovery area where its parachute was deployed. The Firebee was then either retrieved in mid-air by helicopter or recovered from land or water.

FOX AT

ROLE: Reconnaissance and surveillance
COUNTRY: CAC Systems, France

POWER PLANT: 1 x Limbach L 275E piston engine. rated at 22 hp
DIMENSIONS: Span 11.81 ft; length 9.02 ft
WEIGHTS: Empty 143 lb; max. payload 55 lb; max. gross 253.5 lb
PERFORMANCE: Cruising speed 97 kt; ceiling 13,125 ft; max. range 135nm; endurance 5 hours

SENSORS: Fixed or gyrostabilized TV cameras; FLIR; thermal analysers, Linescan 6000 pts-I VHF or radar jammers; NBC sensors
DATA LINK: Real-time uplink and double downlink and tracking antenna
LAUNCH: Ground or ship based bungee or pneumatic launcher
GUIDANCE/TRACKING: Remote control and/or pre-programmed (98 waypoints); INS and differential GPS navigation
RECOVERY: Parachute or belly landing (land or sea)

CUSTOMER: France and undisclosed others

Used for overland reconnaissance over Bosnia during the first half of 1994, Fox AT is one of three basic Fox variants. Fox TX is an electronic warfare version; Fox TS1 and Fox TS3 are aerial gunnery targets.

GNAT 750

ROLE: Reconnaissance/surveillance, target acquisition /designation, communications relay, EW; SIGINT
COUNTRY: General Atomics Aeronautical Systems Inc., USA

POWER PLANT: I x Rotax 582 piston engine, rated at 63 hp; or Rotax 912, rated at 80 hp
DIMENSIONS: Span 35.27 ft; length 1 7.40 ft; height 1.64 ft (excl landing gear)
WEIGHTS: Empty 560 lb; max. payload 140 lb; max. gross 1,140 lb
PERFORMANCE: Loiter speed 60–70 kt; ceiling 25,000 ft; mission radius 2,600 nm; endurance more than 40 hours

SENSOR: Photographic, TV or E-0 camera; FLIR-radar; active and passive ESM; laser range finder/designator; elint communications relay. On-board data storage and/or real-time transmission
DATA LINK: C-band line of sight command uplink; real-time imagery/data downlink
LAUNCHER: Conventional wheeled take-off
GUIDANCE/TRACKING: Pre-programmed and/or remote control
RECOVERY: Conventional wheeled landing

CUSTOMER: US government, Turkish Army. This high endurance UAV is in service with the US government for surveillance and atmospheric research.

HERMES 450

COUNTRY: Silver Arrow, Israel

POWER PLANT: 2 x 25 hp rotary piston engines
DIMENSIONS: Span 33.5 ft; length 20.5 ft
WEIGHTS: Empty 440 lbs; max. gross 1000 lb
PERFORMANCE: Max speed 100+kt; ceiling 25000+ ft; mission radius 500 nm; max. endurance more than 24 hours

SENSOR: Electro-optical camera or FLIR
DATA LINK: Microwave directional control
LAUNCH: Conventional wheeled take-off and landing
GUIDANCE/TRACKING: Innertial

CUSTOMER: Unknown/In development

HERON

ROLE: Long endurance missions, all weather real-time surveillance, SIGINT missions, communications relay, maritime patrol, civil applications
COUNTRY: Israel Aircraft Industries, MALAT Division, Israel

POWER PLANT: 1 x four stroke, turbo-charged piston, 100 hp continuous power. Variable pitch propeller
DIMENSIONS: Span 54.50 ft; length 27.80 ft
WEIGHTS: Max. payload 500 lb; max. gross 2,400 lb. Useful payload (payload plus fuel) 1,100 lb
PERFORMANCE: Max. speed 120 kt; ceiling 35,000 ft; endurance 40 hours

SENSOR: Optronic day and night, radar, Elint, Comint, ESM, communications relay
DATA LINK: Radio command uplink, real time imagery/data downlink
LAUNCH: Wheeled take-off
GUIDANCE/TRACKING: Remote control and/or pre-programmed; GPS navigation
RECOVERY: Wheeled landing with brakes

CUSTOMER: Not stated

Maiden flight took place in October 1994. Flight attitude of 32,000 ft reached in February 1995. Designed for long endurance.

HUNTER

ROLE: Reconnaissance surveillance and target acquisition
COUNTRY: Israel Aircraft Industries, Israel and TRW Inc., USA

POWER PLANT: 2 x Motto Guzzi piston engines, each rated at 68 hp
DIMENSIONS: Span 29.20 ft; length 22.64 ft; height 5.58 ft
WEIGHTS: Empty 1,300 lb; max. payload 250 lb; max. gross 1,600 lb
PERFORMANCE: Max. speed 110 kt; cruising/loiter speed less than 60–80 kt; ceiling 15,000 ft; mission radius 81 nm; endurance 12 hours

SENSORS: IAI Tamam MOSP multi-sensor (options one or two TV cameras, FLIR and TV, and FLIR or TV and laser rangefinder/designator)
LAUNCH: Wheeled take-off (optionally, rocket boost)
DATA LINK: Al Etta C-band real time uplink (two) and downlink (two); provision for onboard imagery/data recording
GUIDANCE/TRACKING: Pre-programmed and/or remote control
RECOVERY: Wheeled landing via hook and arrester cable; parachute for emergency recovery

CUSTOMER: US Army Navy and Marine Corps

Hunter combines an airframe based on the IAI Impact air vehicle with other systems integration by TRWs Avionics and Surveillance Group. In June 1992 it won the USJPO's short-range competition, and is now in low-rate initial production for service entry in 1995.

Ka–37

ROLE: Aerial photography; communications relay; agriculture work; search and rescue; aerial supply
COUNTRY: Kamov OKB, Russia

POWER PLANT: 1 x piston engine, rated at 60 hp
DIMENSIONS: Rotor diameter 15.75 ft; length 9.43 ft; height 5.38 ft
WEIGHTS: Max. payload 110 lb; max. gross 551 lb
PERFORMANCE: Max. speed 59 kt; ceiling 5,200 ft; endurance 45 minutes

SENSORS: Cameras, communications relay or other, to customer's requirements
DATA LINK: Radio command uplink
LAUNCH: Vertical take-off
GUIDANCE/TRACKING: Pre-programmed and/or remote control
RECOVERY: Vertical landing

CUSTOMER: South Korea

A typical Kamov co-axial helicopter, the Ka-37 was undergoing flight trials in 1993. The photograph shows it with external tanks and spraybars in ARCH configuration (Agriculture Remotely Controlled Helicopter), a joint development programme with Daewoo of South Korea.

KETTERING AERIAL TORPEDO 'BUG'

POWER PLANT: One De Palma four-cylinder of 40 hp
DIMENSIONS: span 14.11 ft; length: 12.6 ft; height 4.8 ft
WEIGHT: 530 lb loaded
ARMAMENT: 180 lb of high explosive
PERFORMANCE: Design speed 100 kt; range 75 miles

The Kettering Aerial Torpedo, nicknamed the 'Bug', was invented by Charles F. Kettering of Dayton. It was developed and built by Dayton-Wright Airplane Company in 1918 for the U.S. Army Signal Corps.

The unmanned Bug took off from a dolly which ran along a track. It was stabilized on course toward its target by a system of internal pre-set vacuum pneumatic and electrical controls. After a predetermined length of time, a control closed an electrical circuit which shut off the engine. The wings were then released, causing the Bug to plunge to earth where its 180 pounds of explosive detonated on impact.

Although initial testing was successful, World War One ended before the Bug could enter combat. Fewer than 50 Bugs had been completed at the time of the Armistice. After the war, the Air Service conducted additional tests on the weapon, but scarcity of funds in the 1920s halted further development. The full-size reproduction of the Bug was built by Museum personnel. It was placed on display in 1964.

JAVELIN

ROLE: Reconnaissance
COUNTRY: BAI Aerosystems Inc., USA

POWER PLANT: 1 x 2-stroke or electric engine
DIMENSIONS: Span 8 ft; length 5.7 ft; height 1.7 ft
WEIGHTS: empty 8.7 lb; max. payload 3.2 lb; max gross 20 lb
PERFORMANCE: Max. speed 55 kt; endurance 45 minutes

SENSOR: Stabilized colour pan-tilt zoom TV camera
DATA LINK: 1.8 GHz video with data sideband, 450 MHz uplink
LAUNCHER: Hand
GUIDANCE/TRACKING: GPS/autonavigation
RECOVERY: Conventional

CUSTOMER: In development

Similar to AeroVironment Pointer but heavier and with more power – less susceptible to wind speed

LARK

ROLE: Anti-radar jamming and/or attack; decoy; reconnaissance
COUNTRY: Kentron, Division of Denel (Pty) Ltd, South Africa

POWER PLANT: 1 x Alvis rotary piston engine, rated at 38 hp
DIMENSION: Span 6.89 ft; length 7.98 ft; body diameter 0.89 ft; height 1.80 ft
WEIGHTS: Warhead 44 lb; gross 254.5 lb
PERFORMANCE: Diving speed approx. 343 kt; cruising speed 113 kt, loiter speed 92 kt, ceiling 14,765 ft; mission range 216 nm; loiter time at mission range 2 hours 30 minutes

SENSORS: Nose-mounted radar seeker head (2-1 0 GHz, extendible to 0.7-18 Hz)
DATA LINK: Not stated
LAUNCH: Rocket boost from truck- or ship-mounted container
GUIDANCE/TRACKING: Pre-programmed; GPS-based navigation
RECOVERY: Non-recoverable in attack role; parachute and airbag for other roles

CUSTOMER: Potentially South African armed forces and export

Originally known as ARQ-10, Lark's primary mission is to harass hostile radars with jamming devices or destroy them with its fragmentation HE warhead. It can recover from a terminal dive and return to loiter mode if it loses command signal.

MART MK 11

ROLE: Battlefield reconnaissance, surveillance and target acquisition
COUNTRY: Altec Industries SA, France

POWER PLANT: 1 x TTL WAE 342-30A piston engine, rated at 25 hp
DIMENSIONS: Span 11.15 ft; length 10.58 ft; height 2.33 ft
WEIGHTS: Empty 178.5 lb; max. payload 55 lb; max. gross 242.5 lb
PERFORMANCE: Max. speed 119 kt; cruising/loiter speed 48-65 kt; ceiling 9,850 ft; climb 1,083 ft/min; mission radius 27 to 54 nm; endurance 4 hours

SENSORS: B/W or colour CCD camera; IRLS; LL TV; flares; EGM/ESM
DATA LINK: Radio command uplink; real-time video downlink
LAUNCH: Bungee catapult from trailer-mounted rail
GUIDANCE/TRACKING: Remote control, aided by underwing wide-angle video camera
RECOVERY: Parachute or belly skid

CUSTOMER: French Army

The original MART (Mini-Avion de Reconnaissance Telepilote) formed part of France's Daguet Division during the 1991 Gulf war. In-service MARTS, and subsequent new-production systems, are now to Mkil standard with more accurate GPS navigation, longer-range target acquisition and quieter operation.

MARULA

ROLE: Tactical reconnaissance/surveillance; target acquisition: anti-radar
COUNTRY: SAGEM and Aeronautique et Systemes, France

POWER PLANT: 1 x Alvis rotary piston engine, rated at 38 hp
DIMENSIONS: Span 7.55 ft; length 6.89 ft; height 2.30 ft
WEIGHTS: Empty 88 lb; max. payload 77 lb; max. gross 297.5 lb
PERFORMANCE: Diving speed 270 kt; max. speed 135 kt; loiter speed 97 kt; ceiling 13,125 ft; mission radius 216 nm; max. endurance over 5 hours

SENSORS: Day/night FLIR; EW; radar seeker
DATA LINK: radio control uplink; video and telemetry down links
LAUNCH: Rocket boost from truck-mounted container
GUIDANCE/TRACKING: Pre-programmed or remote control; GPS/INS navigation
RECOVERY: Parachute and airbag

CUSTOMER: Potentially, French armed forces and export

Marula, the evaluation phase of which was completed in early 1994, is a mid-range multi-role UAV. It can be re-programmed in flight, and the large wing endplates are side-force generators that enable it to make flat turns. In the attack role it can carry a pre-fragmented warhead.

MIRACH 26

ROLE: Battlefield surveillance and target acquisition/designation-I EW; communications relay
COUNTRY: Meteor CAE, Italy

POWER PLANT: 1 x Sachs SF 350 piston engine, rated at 27 hp
DIMENSIONS: Span 15.52 ft; length 12.63 ft; height 4.17 ft
WEIGHTS: Empty 410 lb; max. payload 110 lb.
PERFORMANCE: Max. speed 119 kt; loiter speed 78 kt; ceiling 11,480 ft; climb 590 ft/min.; mission radius 54 nm; max. endurance more than 6 hours

SENSORS: E-0 or IR camera; laser range finder; elint, comint; active and passive ESM-1 commune cations relay
DATA LINK: Secure radio command uplink: real-time or delayed imagery/data downlink
LAUNCH: Rocket boost from truck-mounted ramp
GUIDANCE/TRACKING: Pre-programmed and/or remote control; GPS/auto pilot navigation
RECOVERY: Parachute and ventral fin

CUSTOMER: Italian Army

Mirach 26 is the definitive version of the earlier Mirach 20, of which a prototype system was delivered to the Italian Army in 1988. Operational evaluation of an eight-air-vehicle Mirach 26 system began in 1994, forming the SORAO component at the Italian Army's CATRIN Corps-level communications intelligence system.

OQ-2A

ROLE: Aerial Target
COUNTRY: Radioplane, USA

ENGINE: 1+ O-15-1 2-cylinder, air-cooled, simultaneously firing, 2-cycle of 6 hp
DIMENSIONS: Span 13 ft 3 in; length 8 ft 8 in; height 2 ft 8 in
WEIGHT: 108 lb maximum
PERFORMANCE: Maximum speed 90 mph; endurance 60 minutes; service ceiling 8,000 ft

In the mid-1930s, radio-controlled model airplanes became the basis for the Army Air Corps' development of the aerial targets for antiaircraft gunnery training. The OQ-2A was successful enough to generate contracts for almost 1,000 targets in 1943.

The OQ-2A was catapult-launched and was recovered under a 24-foot diameter parachute. Conventional landing gear cushioned the landing impact.

OUTRIDER

ROLE: Surveillance and target acquisition;
COUNTRY: Alliant Techsystems Inc., USA

POWER PLANT: 1 x McCulloch 4318F 4 cyl./pusher
DIMENSIONS: Span 11.1 ft; length 9.32 ft
WEIGHTS: Empty 140 lb; max. payload 50 lb; max.
gross 425 lb
PERFORMANCE: Max speed 120 kt; loiter speed 57
kt; radius of action 125 miles; ceiling 15,000 ft;
climb more than 2,000 ft/min.; endurance 4+ hours
at 125 miles

SENSORS: Daylight TV, FLIR
DATA LINK: Radio command uplink; real-time
imagery/data downlink
LAUNCH: 300 ft unimproved strip
GUIDANCE/TRACKING: Pre-programmed
RECOVERY: Auto wheel landing, parachute
emergency

CUSTOMER: US Armed Forces, 24, Tactical
Unmanned Aerial Vehicle Manoeuvre (TUAV)
ACTD plus up to 244 more

Derived from the 'Twinwing' developed by
Mission Technologies. The Outrider beat nine
competing designs to win the Joint UAV
programme and is manufactured by Alliant
Techsystems Inc., USA.
Each Outrider system consists of four dual-wing
air vehicles, their mission payloads, associated
ground control equipment, a Global Positioning
System launch and recovery system, and a remote
terminal to provide payload information to the
field commander. The complete system, which fits
inside two HUMVEEs and a trailer, can be
transported in a single C-130 aircraft

PATHFINDER

ROLE: Solar-powered research
COUNTRY: AeroVironment Inc., USA

POWER PLANT: B x brushless, permanent magnet
electric motors, total output 1.5 kW
DIMENSIONS: Span 98.40 ft; wing chord 8 ft
WEIGHTS: Payload approx 88 lb; gross 540 lb
PERFORMANCE: Cruising speed 31 kt IAS; ceiling
70,000 ft

SENSORS: Solar array panels with max. power
capacity of 2.8-8.0 kW
DATA LINK: Radio command uplink; system status
telemetry downlink
LAUNCH: Wheeled take-off
GUIDANCE/TRACKING: Remote control (altitude
and heading commands, 11 angle and motor rpm
adjustment)
RECOVERY: Wheeled landing

CUSTOMER: Research for BMDO Raptor
programme

Pathfinder was originally built in 1983 as a high-
altitude, long-endurance platform called HALSOL
(high Altitude Solar), but was upgraded in recent
years to develop a possible solar power package as
a propulsion for the Raptor UAV. First flight was
in October 1993.

PERSEUS

ROLE: Atmospheric research
COUNTRY: Aurora Flight Sciences, USA

POWER PLANT: 1 x turbocharged piston engine, rated at 80 hp
DIMENSIONS: Span 58.73 ft; length approx 26.74 ft
WEIGHTS: Empty 992 lb; max. payload 441 lb; max. gross 2,205 lb
PERFORMANCE: Ceiling 65,600 ft; max. endurance 24 hours

SENSORS: Variable, to customer's requirements; can include dropsondes, hygrometers and particle measuring probes
DATA LINK: UHF radio command uplink
LAUNCH: Wheeled take-off with aero-tow
GUIDANCE/TRACKING: Not stated
RECOVERY: Wheeled landing

CUSTOMER: NASA (Perseus A); Sandia National Laboratories (Perseus B)

A Perseus technology demonstrator first flew in November 1991, followed in December 1993 by the first of two Perseus As for NASA. Perseus B, to which the specification data apply, was developed for missions on behalf of the US Department of Energy.

PHOENIX

ROLE: Battlefield surveillance, target acquisition and artillery fire adjustment
COUNTRY: GEC-Marconi Avionics Ltd, UK

POWER PLANT: 1 x TTL WAE 342 piston engine, rated at 25 hp
DIMENSIONS: Span 18.04 ft
WEIGHTS: Max. payload 110 lb; max. gross 386 lb
PERFORMANCE: Max. 90 kt; endurance 5 hours

SENSORS: Turret-mounted IR in ventral pod
DATA LINK: Narrow-beam J-band command uplink; real-time imagery downlink
LAUNCH: Truck-mounted pneumatic/hydraulic catapult
GUIDANCE/TRACKING: Pre-programmed (autonomous launch and fully automatic manoeuvres)
RECOVERY: Parachute and impact-absorbing dorsal fairing

CUSTOMER: British Army

Phoenix was developed to a British Army specification to provide surveillance, target acquisition and shot adjustment for MLRS and other depth fire artillery. The underslung payload pod is roll stabilized to provide a level platform during all air vehicle manoeuvres.

PIONEER

ROLE: Surveillance
COUNTRY: Pioneer UAV, USA

POWER PLANT: 1 x Sachs SF 350 piston engine, rated at 26 hp
DIMENSIONS: Span 16.76 ft; length 13.98 ft
WEIGHTS: Max. payload 99 lb; max. gross 419 lb
PERFORMANCE: Max. speed 95 kt; loiter speed 60 kt; ceiling 12,000 ft; climb 800ft/min.; endurance 5 hours 30 minutes

SENSORS: TADIRAN Moked 200 TV camera or Moked 400 FLIR standard
DATA LINK: Radio command uplink; real-time or delayed imagery/data downlink
LAUNCH: Wheeled take-off, catapult or rocket boost
GUIDANCE/'TRACKING: Pre-programmed and/or remote control
RECOVERY: Wheeled landing with hook and arrester wire on landing; net for shipboard operation

CUSTOMER: US Army, Navy and Marine corps

A veteran of Persian Gulf operations since 1988, Pioneer was acquired originally in 1985. Pending the introduction of the BOM-155A Hunter, the Pioneer is expected to remain in US Navy service until at least 1999, serving aboard LPD amphibious transport vessels instead of battleships as hitherto.

POINTER D-2

ROLE: Close-range surveillance and target acquisition
COUNTRY: AeroVironment Inc., USA

POWER PLANT: 1 x electric motor, rated at 300W; powered by two lithium or nickel-cadmium batteries
DIMENSIONS: Span 9.00 ft; length 6.00 ft
WEIGHTS: Max. payload 2 lb; max. gross 8 lb
PERFORMANCE: Max speed 43 kt, cruising/loiter speed 19 kt, ceiling 985 ft, climb 610 ft/min, control radius 4.3 nm, endurance 20 minutes (nickel-cadmium) or 1 hour 15 minutes (lithium)

SENSORS: B/W, colour or LL TV camera standard; FLIR or chemical agent detector optional
DATA LINK: Radio control uplink; real-time video downlink
LAUNCH: Hand-launched
GUIDANCE/TRACKING: Remote control; GPS navigation optional
RECOVERY: Engine shutdown, then deep stall to belly landing

CUSTOMER: US Army, Marine Corps and National Guard (FOM-151A)

This man-portable miniature sailplane can be dismantled and carried, with its ground operators' radio control and imagery receiving equipment, in two backpacks with a combined weight of only 75 lb (34 kg).

PREDATOR

ROLE: Reconnaissance and target acquisition
COUNTRY: General Atomics, USA

POWER PLANT: 1 x Rotax 912 piston engine, rated at 80 hp, turbocharge option
DIMENSIONS: Span 48.40 ft; length 26.70ft; height 3.17 ft (excl landing gear)
WEIGHTS: Empty 980 lb; max. payload 450 lb; max. gross 2,080 lb
PERFORMANCE: Loiter speed 60 kt; ceiling 25,000 ft; mission radius over 3,000 nm; max. endurance over 24 hours

SENSORS: Film or TV camera; synthetic aperture radar; FLIR; IRLS; elint/comint; active and passive ESM; laser range finder/designator; comms relay
DATA LINK: radio command uplink (C-band within line-of-sight, UHF and KU-band satellite beyond); real-time imagery/data downlink
LAUNCH: Conventional wheeled take-off
GUIDANCE/TRACKING: Pre-programmed and/or remote control; GPS/INS navigation
RECOVERY: Conventional wheeled landing

CUSTOMER: US Department of Defense

Derived from the Gnat 750, DARPA designation 'Tier 2', Predator's job was developed under an ACTD programme but now has reached production and is fully operational for tactical endurance missions. Ten have been ordered for operational use; the first example flew in June 1994.

RANGER

ROLE: Reconnaissance and surveillance
COUNTRY: Oerlikon-Contraves, Switzerland

POWER PLANT: 1 x Gobler-Hirth F-31 piston engine, rated at 38 hp
DIMENSIONS: Span 18.7 ft; length 15.1 ft; height 3.7 ft
WEIGHTS: Max. payload 86 lb; max. gross 595 lb
PERFORMANCE: Max. speed 119 kt; ceiling 15,000 ft; mission radius 62 nm; max. endurance 5 hours

SENSORS: Different payload configurations available such as: TV, FLIR, FLIR and TV, TV with laser designator, FLIR with laser designator
DATA LINK: Microwave-band primary and UHF-band secondary uplink; microwave-band video and telemetry downlinks
LAUNCH: From hydraulic catapult with rails
GUIDANCE/TRACKING: Pre-programmed and/or remote controlled
RECOVERY: Three-point wheeled landing with arrester wire, or triple skids; parachute for emergency recovery

CUSTOMER: Swiss Army

Ranger was developed for the Swiss government with the assistance of Israel Aircraft Industries.

RAPTOR

ROLE: Boost phase interception of theatre ballistic missiles
COUNTRY: Scaled Composites Inc., USA

POWER PLANT: 1 x Rotax 912 turbocharged piston engine, low altitude configuration max. power 80 hp, high altitude configuration >25hp at 65,000 ft
DIMENSIONS: Span 66 ft; length 25 ft
WEIGHTS (approx): Empty 810 lb; min. payload 150 lb; max. gross 1,800 lb
PERFORMANCE: Ceiling over 65,000 ft (19,810 m); endurance 48 hours; max speed 247 kt at 65,000 ft; climb speed 55 kt

SENSORS: IR launch detection and tracking cameras (MWIR waveband)
DATA LINK: Not stated
LAUNCH: Cradle on top of HMMWV or similar ground vehicle; possible options include tow launch or rocket boost
GUIDANCE/TRACKING: Remote control
RECOVERY: Engine shutdown and glide to skid landing; retractable wheel gear under consideration

CUSTOMER: US Ballistic Missile Defense Organisation

Raptor (Responsive Aircraft Program for Theatre Operations) is designed for long-endurance monitoring of hostile ballistic missile sites, carrying Talon hypersonic missiles to destroy them within seconds of launch. The Raptor demonstrator made its first unmanned flight in December 1993.

RAVEN

ROLE: Surveillance and reconnaissance
COUNTRY: Flight Refuelling Ltd, UK

POWER PLANT: 1 x Sachs Dolmar piston engine, rated at 13 hp
DIMENSIONS: Span 11.81 ft; length 10.50 ft; height 2.71 ft
WEIGHTS: Zero fuel 164 lb; max. payload 38 lb; max. tow 185 lb
PERFORMANCE: Max. speed 110 kt; loiter speed 48 kt; ceiling 14,000 ft; mission radius 54 nm; max. endurance 4 hours

SENSORS: Daylight or LL TV; FLIR or other
DATA LINK: Radio command uplink; real-time video downlink
LAUNCH: Bungee catapult from trailer-mounted rail
GUIDANCE/TRACKING: Remote control and/or pre-programmed; GPS-based navigation
RECOVERY: Parachute or belly skid

CUSTOMER: None announced, but widely evaluated

Raven is a Flight Refuelling development of XRAE-1, an experimental UAV designed and tested by the former Royal Aircraft Establishment, Farnborough. After several stages of refinement, it is now a fully proven tactical surveillance system, incorporating GPS navigation and interchangeable payload capability. Several countries are now considering the requirements for a Brigade-level UAV system.

RPO MIDGET

ROLE: Brigade level reconnaissance, surveillance, artillery correction electronic warfare
COUNTRY: TechMent AB, Sweden

POWER PLANT: 13 hp two stroke, benzine
DIMENSIONS: Rotor diameter 6.56 ft; length 5.9 ft; width 4.5 ft; height 3.1 ft
WEIGHTS: Take-off 99.20 lb; payload 44,10 lb
PERFORMANCE: Endurance 3–4 hours; speed range 18.6–80.8 mph; range 62.1 miles

SENSORS: Non-stabilized and stabilized camera platforms. CCD or infrared downward-looking cameras. Forward-looking wide-angle CCD pilot camera.
DATA LINK: L-band 1.0-2.0 Hz 3-1 0 waft, Multiplex system for two analogue video channels (observation camera and pilot camera). Range 62.1 miles
LAUNCH: Jump start 4 ft, wheeled take-off 33–66 ft
GUIDANCE/TRACKING: GPS and inertial navigation.
RECOVERY: Wheeled landing less than 10 m; Set angle 45 degrees

CUSTOMER: Under development for Swedish Army

The RPG gyroplane incorporates elements of a fixed-wing aeroplane and helicopter. The gyrocopter meets most of the demands a brigade and battalion observation system has to fulfil.

SEAMOS

ROLE: Maritime surveillance; OTH target acquisition/designation; other maritime roles
COUNTRY: Deutsche Aerospace (Dornier), Germany

POWER PLANT: 1 x Allison 25O-C2OW turboshaft: 420 shp
DIMENSIONS: Rotor diameter 20.01 ft; length 9.35 ft; width 5.09 ft; height 8.29
WEIGHTS: Empty 1,367 lb; max. payload 308.50 lb; max. gross 2,337 lb
PERFORMANCE: Max. speed 90 kt; ceiling 13,125 ft; endurance up to 4 hours

SENSORS: Radar of E-0
DATA LINK: Radio command uplink; real-time imagery/data downlink
LAUNCH: Vertical take-off
GUIDANCE/TRACKING: Pre-programmed; GPS/INS navigation
RECOVERY: Vertical landing

CUSTOMER: Under development for German Navy; also candidate for US and NATO maritime requirements

Seamos (See-Autklarungs MiRel und Ortungs System: Maritime reconnaissance and detection system) shared, with the cancelled land-based Geamos, a history of Dornier rotary-wing UAV development dating from the Do 32U and Kiebitz programmes of the 1970s. A modified Gyrodyne OH-50D has served as a proof-of-concept demonstrator.

SEARCHER

ROLE: Long-endurance surveillance and target acquisition
COUNTRY: Israel Aircraft Industries, Malat Division, Israel

POWER PLANT: 47 hp
DIMENSIONS: Span 25.1 ft; length 16.7 ft; height 4.1 ft
WEIGHTS: Max. payload 150 lb; max. gross 880 lb
PERFORMANCE: Max. speed 110 kt; loiter speed 60 kt; ceiling 17,000 ft, max. endurance 12 hours

SENSORS: TV camera; FLIR
DATA LINK: Radio command uplink (primary and backup); real-time video downlink
LAUNCH: Wheeled take-off
GUIDANCE/TRACKING: Pre-programmed and/or remote control
RECOVERY: Wheeled landing with hook and arresting cable on land; net for shipboard operation

CUSTOMER: Israel and other undisclosed armed forces

Entered service in mid-1992. Searcher greatly expanded the capability offered by Mastiff and Scout. More survivable by virtue of redundant sub-systems, it can stay airborne for much longer, can acquire targets by its surveillance sensors, and downlink data in real-time.

SEEKER

ROLE: Reconnaissance, target acquisition and artillery fire correction; communications relay
COUNTRY: Kentron Division of Denel (Pty) Ltd, South Africa

POWER PLANT: 1 x piston engine, rated at 50 hp
DIMENSIONS: Span 22.97 ft; length 14.53 ft; height 4.27 ft
WEIGHTS: Empty 342 lb; max. payload 88 lb; max. gross 562 lb
PERFORMANCE: Max. speed 120 kt IAS; loiter speed 65 kt IAS; ceiling over 18,000 ft; climb 1,000 ft/min; mission radius 108 nm; max. endurance over 12 hours (9 with max payload)

SENSORS: Daylight colour or LL TV camera; FLIR; communications relay, meteorological, chemical detection
DATA LINK: 0-band radio command uplink with UHF backup; real-time imagery/data downlink
LAUNCH: Wheeled take-off standard; winch assistance optional
GUIDANCE/TRACKING: Remote control and/or pre-programmed; autonomous return-to base provision
RECOVERY: Wheeled landing and arrester wire

CUSTOMER: South African Defence Force (Air Force and Army); Chilean Army; others

Used operationally by the SADF during the war in Angola, Seeker was developed by the former Armscor after earlier experience of operating the Israeli Scout UAV. It first flew in 1986 and entered SADF service in 1987.

SENTINEL

ROLE: Reconnaissance, surveillance and target acquisition/designation; EW; communications relay
COUNTRY: Bombardier Inc, Canadair, Defence Systems Division, Canada

POWER PLANT: 1 x Williams International WTS34-16 turboshaft, rated at 51.5 shp being upgraded to WTS-125 turboshaft
DIMENSIONS: Rotor diameter 9.19 ft; max. body diameter 2.1 ft; height 5.38 ft
WEIGHTS: Empty 220 lb; payload 75–99 lb; max. gross 419 lb
PERFORMANCE: Max. speed 77 kt; ceiling 9,840 ft; climb rate programmable for 394 to 787 ft/min; typical mission radius 32.5 nm; max. endurance 3.5 hours

SENSORS: TV camera; FLIR; communications relays; active EW
DATA LINK: Radio command uplink; real-time video downlink
LAUNCH: Automated vertical take-off
GUIDANCE/TRACKING: Remote control (GPS)
RECOVERY: Vertical landing; decklock for maritime operation (automatic)

CUSTOMER: Evaluated for US Navy, NATO and other close-range land-based and maritime requirements

Since its first tethered flight in August 1978 the CL-227 Sentinel has become a much more capable UAV. Its most recent upgrade is to a Williams International WTS-125 turboshaft (Heavy Fuel Engine) capable of 125 hp.

SHADOW 200

ROLE: Reconnaissance, surveillance, target acquisition, battle damage assessment and artillery adjustment
COUNTRY: AAI Corporation, USA

POWER PLANT: 1 x UAV Engines Ltd, 741 Rotary (gasoline), 37 hp; 1 x AHF - 12 Rotary (diesel) 25 hp
DIMENSIONS: Span 12.75 ft; length 9.0 ft
WEIGHTS: Empty 170 lb; max. payload 50 lb; max. gross 230 lb
PERFORMANCE: Max. speed 150 kt; cruise 84 kt; ceiling 15,000 ft; endurance 3+ hours

SENSORS: TV, FLIR, meteorological
DATA LINK: Range 31 miles
LAUNCH: Rail or wheel
GUIDANCE/TRACKING: Pre-programmed, remote control, navigation by GPS, data link or dead reckoning
RECOVERY: Net or wheel

CUSTOMER: Candidate for Joint Tactical UAV-Manoeuvre Variant

The Shadow 200 has an inverted-V tail and slimmer fuselage than the Shadow 600. It is a candidate in the current US Joint Tactical UAV-Manoeuvre competition.

SHADOW 600

ROLE: Reconnaissance and target acquisition; EW; communications relay
COUNTRY: AAI Corp., USA

POWER PLANT: 1 x UAV Engines Ltd, S01 Rotary Engine, rated at 52 hp
DIMENSIONS: Span 22.40 ft; length 15,40 ft; height 4.00 ft
WEIGHTS: Empty 360 lb; max. payload 100 lb; max. gross 600 lb
PERFORMANCE: Max. speed 115 kt; cruising speed 73 kt; ceiling 17,000 ft; mission radius 108 nm; data link max. range 108 nm; endurance over 14 hours

SENSORS: TV or E-0 (LL TV) camera; FLIR; passive ESM; communications relay; meteorological; chemical detection
DATA LINK: AAI Spread spectrum of clear command uplink; real-time imagery/data downlink; provision for onboard data recording and storage, data link range 120 m
LAUNCH: Wheeled take-off
GUIDANCE/TRACKING: Pre-programmed and/or remote control; navigation by GPS or data link AZEL or dead reckoning
RECOVERY: Wheeled landing

CUSTOMER: Various international customers who will not release data

Shadow 600, ordered by Turkey in 1994, is the largest member of AAI's current Shadow family.

SHMEL

ROLE: Battlefield surveillance; EW
COUNTRY: AS Yakovlev OKB, Russia

POWER PLANT: 1 x Samara/Trud (Kuznetsov) P-032 piston engine, rated at 32 hp
DIMENSIONS: Span 10.66 ft; length 9.12 ft; height 3.61 ft
WEIGHTS: Max. payload 154 lb; max. gross 287 lb
PERFORMANCE: Max. speed 97 kt; ceiling 9,850 ft; mission radius 32.5 nm; endurance 2 hours

SENSORS: Daylight TV camera; IRLS; EW jammer
DATA LINK: Radio command uplink; real-time video downlink
LAUNCH: Container launch by rocket boost from vehicle-mounted rail
GUIDANCE/TRACKING: Remote control
RECOVERY: Parachute or parafoil and landing logs

CUSTOMER: Soviet Army/Russian; Syria

The Yak-61 Shmel-1 (Bumblebee) is the air vehicle component of the Sterkh tactical reconnaissance system, carried in a container atop a BTR D tracked armoured vehicle which also accommodates the launch rail and control station. It entered Soviet Army service in 1990 and was ordered by Syria in 1992.

SPERWER

ROLE: Tactical reconnaissance, surveillance, target acquisition
COUNTRY: SAGEM SA, France

POWER PLANT: 70hp 2-stroke engine
DIMENSIONS: Span 13.5 ft
WEIGHTS: Payload capacity 100 lb
PERFORMANCE: Max. speed 135 kt; loiter speed 65 kt; ceiling 17000 ft; mission range 120 miles

SENSORS: FLIR camera
DATA LINK: Near real-time video downlink
GUIDANCE/TRACKING: Pre-programmed; navigation; INS and GPS
RECOVERY: Parachute and airbag

CUSTOMER: Royal Netherlands Army

TIER II- (MINUS) GLOBAL HAWK

ROLE: Reconnaissance/surveillance
COUNTRY: Teledyne Ryan Aeronautical Inc., USA

POWER PLANT: I x Allison Rolls Royce AE3007H turbofan at 7,050 lb thrust
DIMENSIONS: Span 116.2 ft; length 44.4 ft; height 15.2 ft
WEIGHTS: Empty 8,940 lb; max. payload 2000 lb; max. gross 22,914 lb; fuel 14,700 lb
PERFORMANCE: Speed 350 kt; ceiling 65,000+ ft; mission radius 3000 nm; range 14,500 miles; endurance more than 42 hours

SENSOR: E-O, IR and SAR; active and passive ESM; on-board data storage and/or real-time transmission
DATA LINK: Radio command uplink (X-band within line-of-sight, UHF and KU-band satellite beyond); real-time imagery/data downlink
LAUNCHER: Conventional wheeled take-off, 5,000 ft
GUIDANCE/TRACKING: Pre-programmed/Autonomous
RECOVERY: Conventional wheeled landing, 5,000 ft

CUSTOMER: USAF 2

TIER III- (MINUS) DARKSTAR

ROLE: Reconnaissance/surveillance
COUNTRY: Lockheed Martin Skunk
Works/Boeing, USA

POWER PLANT: 1 x Williams FJ-44-1A turbofan at
1,900 lb
DIMENSIONS: Span 69 ft; length 15 ft; height 5 ft
WEIGHTS: Empty 4,360 lb; max. payload 1000 lb;
max. gross 8,600 lb; fuel 3,240 lb
PERFORMANCE: Speed 250+ kt; ceiling 45,000+ ft;
mission radius 500+ nm; range 4,000+ miles;
endurance more than 8 hours at 500 miles
SENSOR: E-O, IR or SAR; active and passive ESM;
on-board data storage and/or real-time
transmission
DATA LINK: Radio command uplink X-band
within line-of-sight, UHF and KU-band satellite
beyond); real-time imagery/data downlink

LAUNCHER: Conventional wheeled take-off, 4,000 ft
GUIDANCE/TRACKING: Pre-programmed/
Autonomous
RECOVERY: Conventional wheeled landing, 4,000 ft

CUSTOMER: USAF 4

Utilizing technology which was reported derived
from the cancelled Tier III program the ultra
stealthy DarkStar performed its first flight in May
1996. However, its second flight was short-lived
and dramatic as the vehicle went out of control
and crashed just off the runway at Edwards AFB.

TRA MODEL 154/AQM-91A

COUNTRY: Teledyne Ryan Aeronautical, USA

POWER PLANT: 1 x General Electric YJ-97-GE-3
Turbojet 4000 lb thrust
DIMENSIONS: Span 47.68 ft; length 34.2 ft
WEIGHTS: Empty 3800 lbs, max gross 5400
PERFORMANCE: Max. speed 440+kt; ceiling 78000+
ft; mission radius 1900 nm; max. endurance more
than 4 hours

SENSOR: Optical camera
DATA LINK: Microwave directional control
LAUNCH: Air launched DC-130E
GUIDANCE/TRACKING: Innertial
RECOVERY: Parachute with either MARS Mid-Air
Helicopter or ground with airbags

CUSTOMER: USAF (38 inc. prototypes)

UAOS

ROLE: Battlefield surveillance, target acquisition and artillery fire adjustment, comms relay
COUNTRY: Advanced Technologies & Engineering Co. (Pty) Ltd (ATE), South Africa

POWER PLANT: 1 x piston engine, rated at 22 hp
DIMENSIONS: Span 16.60 ft; length 9.45 ft; height 2.72 ft
WEIGHTS: Max. payload 81.60 lb; gross 275.60 lb
PERFORMANCE: Max. speed 108 kt; ceiling 16,500 ft; endurance over 3 hours; mission radius 32.5 nm

SENSORS: Daylight Monochrome TV camera, FLIR, comms relay
DATA LINK: Real-time video downlink and two-way data link
LAUNCH: Bungee catapult from vehicle-mounted rail
GUIDANCE/TRACKING: Full autonomous pre-programmable mission (optional semi-automatic remote control capability)
RECOVERY: Parachute and frangible belly skid

CUSTOMER: South African Army (artillery)

ATE is contracted by the SA Army for development and production of the UAOS system, as part of the AS2000 artillery engagement system. First flight of XDM air vehicle took place on 16 March 1995. Delivery of first production system is scheduled for early 1997.

UAV–X1

ROLE: Short-range reconnaissance and surveillance
COUNTRY: Tusas Aerospace Industries, TAI, Turkey

POWER PLANT: 1 x Norten NR-801 rated at 42 hp
DIMENSIONS: Span 19.6 ft; length 13.1 ft; height 16.3 ft
WEIGHTS: Empty 330 lb; max. payload 100lb; max. gross 540 lb
PERFORMANCE: Max. speed 120 kt; ceiling 15,000 ft
SENSOR: Daylight TV
DATA LINK: Radio command uplink; real-time video downlink
LAUNCHER: Conventional wheeled take-off
GUIDANCE/TRACKING: Remote control, GPS navigation option
RECOVERY: Conventional wheeled landing

CUSTOMER: In development

Turkey's first experimental short-range UAV

W570A

ROLE: High altitude endurance UAV for a range of missions including intelligence, surveillance and reconnaissance
COUNTRY: Frontier Systems Inc., USA

POWER PLANT: 2 x Williams Int. FJ44-2 turbofans, each rated at 2300 lb of thrust
DIMENSIONS: Span 160 ft; length 25 ft; ground clearance 6 ft; wing area 1350 sq ft
WEIGHTS: Empty 7000 lb; max. payload 10000 lb; max. take off 26000 lb to 45000 lb
PERFORMANCE: Max. speed Mach 0.7; cruise/loiter speed Mach 0.5 to 0.65; ceiling 70000 ft; endurance 60 hours; range 18000 nm
SENSORS: Long range radars EO/IR sensors; SIGINT
DATA LINK: Suite of multiple data links, both line of sight and SATCOM of up to 500 mbits/sec from VHF to Ku-band
LAUNCH: Conventional taxi and runway take-off; automatic take off; retractable landing gear
GUIDANCE/TRACKING: Triple redudundant GPS/INS and avionics system; autonomous operation and operator-intervention models
RECOVERY: Conventional runway landing, automatic landing

CUSTOMERS: In development

X-36

COUNTRY: NASA/McDonnell Douglas, USA

POWER PLANT: 1 x Williams turbofan of 700 lb thrust
DIMENSIONS: Span 14.4 ft; length 18.2 ft
WEIGHTS: Empty 1090 lb; max. gross approx. 1270 lb
PERFORMANCE: Max. speed 300+ kt; ceiling 20000+ ft

SENSOR: Electro-optical camera in nose for pilot
DATA LINK: N/A
LAUNCH/RECOVERY: Conventional wheeled

CUSTOMER: NASA (2) For development of fighter technology

EXCERPTS FROM THE DARPA MISHAP REPORT

Air Vehicle #1 experienced a porpoising motion during its second takeoff roll, resulting in air vehicle instability at rotation speed. Immediately after liftoff, the air vehicle pitched up to an extremely nose-high attitude, stalled, rolled left and impacted the ground adjacent to the runway. The crash area was entirely within the airfield boundary and on government property. There were no injuries, and no damage was done to private property. The air vehicle, although a major loss, still had some salvageable parts. Weather was not a factor.

The forward fuselage section with two fuel tanks was severely damaged due to ground impact and subsequent fire. In the aft fuselage section, the right side sustained greater damage than the left side. The right main strut area was severely damaged, but the left main wheel well was intact and the left landing gear appeared to be in good condition.

The left wing broke into several pieces upon impact. The right wing remained attached, although rotated 180 degrees and angled to aft. The right wing root area was severely burned and its composite skin delaminated. The root area was severely burned and its composite skin delaminated. The positions of the left and right wing flight control surfaces (ruddevons and elevons) were unknown. All flight control actuators sustained some structural damage. The left side avionics bay (containing the on-board flight computers and communications equipment) was intact and blackened with some metallic cable connectors melted, but it was not opened. The right side payload/sensor bay forward bulkhead and lower panel were

completely destroyed and the pallet (containing the on-board flight telemetry data recorder) was ejected. Although the recorder remained on the pallet, its case was damaged and loose in places with internal components broken, including its 8 millimeter tape. A piece of tape was left in the recorder heads, but efforts to recover its data were unsuccessful.

The engine remained in its compartment, although some engine mounts were damaged and the entire intake was destroyed. The exhaust area, however, appeared to be intact with little impact or fire damage. The engine appeared to have been running/rotating at impact.

The air vehicle was constructed largely of composite material, and carbon-fiber contamination was a potential hazard to personnel responding to the accident scene. Health and safety personnel locked down this hazard by applying a liquid encapsulating solution to the wreckage before it was covered with poly sheeting and canvas tarps. Encapsulant and poly sheeting were again used to control fiber release when the wreckage was loaded on a flatbed truck and moved to a hangar to facilitate the investigation. The unsalvageable remains were later sealed in a large leak-proof container and buried on the base.

INTERNET SITES

DARO Home Page
http://www.acq.osd.mil/daro/

Joint Projects UAV Home Page
http://wwwjtuav.redstone.army.mil/

New Vista Study
http://www.fie.com/fedix/vista.html

UAV Battle Lab
http://www.wg53.eglin.af.mil/battlelab/contact.html

USAF Photos
http://www.dtic.dla.mil/airforcelink/photos/jccc.html

FAS Home Page
http://www.fas.org/irp/imint/predator.htm

ERAST Home Page
http://news.dfrc.nasa.gov/Projects/ERAST/ERAST.html

NASA Photos Home Page
http://www.dfrc.nasa.gov/PhotoServer/index.html

AUVSI Home Page
http://www.erols.com/auvsicc/index.html

DARPA DarkStar Home Page
http://www.darpa.mil/asto/tier3/tier3.html

DARPA Home Page
http://www.arpa.mil/

General Atomics Home Page
http://www.ga.com/asi/aero.html

Teledyne Ryan Home Page
http://www.tdyryan.com/

Lockheed Martin Home Page
http://www.lmco.com/library/

Lockheed Martin Photos Home Page
http://www.lmco.com/photo/a-z.html

Scaled Composites Home Page
http://www.scaled.com/

Boeing DarkStar Home Page
http://www.boeing.com/dsg.darkstar.html

Boeing HeliWing Home Page
http://www.boeing.com/dsg.heliwing.html

Kentron Home Page (RSA)
http://www.denel.co.za/kentron/

WIRED UAV Article
http://www.hotwired.com/wired/4.03/robotplane/

Janes UAV
http://www.thomson.com/janes/uav.html

Aircraft Locator Home Page
http://www.brooklyn.cuny.edu/rec/air/museums/types/q/q.html

Israeli UAV
http://shani.co.il/NewsGuide/news/avi/uav.html

Personel UAV Links
http://members.aol.com/Leoglovka/uav.html

Alliant Outrider Homepage
http://www.atk.com/business/defence/Feature/default.htm

Israeli UAV Simulation Company
http://www.bvr.co.il/text/uav.html

UAVs: See Everything from the Sky
http://www.indigo-net.com/dossiers/359.htm

Raptor D-2 Photos
http://www-phys.llnl.gov/clementine/ATP/DEM2s.gif

Aerospace Review
http://206.43.192.113/news/196/news/weapons.htm

CARS Automated Landing System
http://www.cecer.army.mil/facts/sheets/PL35.html

STM-5B
http://www.s-tec.com/uav/

The ARM (Atmospheric Radiation Measurement)/UAV
(Unmanned Aerospace Vehicle) Program
http://albedo.larc.nasa.gov:1123/uav.html

Pioneer Simulation
http://slice.nosc.mil/coaster/VirtualEnv/Pioneer.html

UAV Research at the University of Sydney in Australia
http://www.ae.su.oz.au/wwwdocs/uav1096.html

Build your Own UAV
http://www.polycosmos.org/robotgrp/roboblmp/
roboblmp.htm

Georgia Tech. Research
http://www.cc.gatech.edu/ai/robot-lab/research/uav.html

USAF Museum
http://www.wpafb.af.mil/museum/index.htm

Ballistic Missile Defense Organisation
http://www.acq.osd.mil/bmdo/bmdolink/html

Chinese UAV
http://www.gsprint.com/cmd/uav.htm

Mystery Aircraft inc. A-12
http://www.fas.org/irp/mystery/history.htm#36

X-36 Photos
http://www.dfrc.nasa.gov/PhotoServer/X-36/index.html

Aviation Week Group
http://www.awgnet.com/

UAV related US DoD news
http://www.dtic.dla.mil/cgi-
bin/waisgate?WAISdbName=/wais/indexes/defenselink/
all&WAISqueryString= UAV

Area-51 Research
http://www.unfomind.com/org/

Private UAV homepage
http://www.greatbasin.com/-daveh/uav/index.html

FreeWing Company
http://www.freewing.com/

1997 International Aerial Robotics Competition
http://avdil.gtri.gatech.edu/AUVS/IARCLaunchPoint.html

Georgia Tech. Micro UAV Flapping Vehicle
http://avdil.gtri.gatech.edu/RCM/RCM/Entomopter/
EntomopterProject.html

Australian Miniature Robotic Aircraft for Long-range
Environmental Monitoring
http://www.bom.gov.au/bmrc/meso/Project/Aerosonde/
aerodev.htm

INDEX

G

H

I

W

X

Y

Z

ABBREVIATIONS

AACU	Anti-Aircraft Co-operation Unit
ACC	Air Combat Command
ACTD	Advanced Concept Technology Demonstration
ADR	Air Data Relay
AFB	Air Force Base
AFLC	Air Force Logistics Command
AI	Air Interdiction
ALARM	Advanced Long-Range Anti-Radiation Missile
ALCM	Air-Launched Cruise Missile
ARPA	Advanced Research Projects Agency
AT	Aerial Target
AV	Air Vehicle
AVEN	Advanced Vectoring Engine Nozzle
AWACS	Airborne Warning and Control System
BDA	Battle Damage Assessment
BMDO	Ballistic Missile Defense Organization
CATA	Control, Automation and Task Allocation
CCD	Charged Couple Device
CDL	Common Data Link
CGS	Common Ground Segment
CIA	Central Intelligence Agency
CIC	Combat Information Center
COMMINT	Communications Intelligence
CONV HAV	Conventional High Altitude Vehicle
DARO	Defense Airborne Reconnaissance Office
DARPA	Defense Advanced Research Projects Agency
DASH	Drone Anti-Submarine Helicopter

DECM	Defensive Electronic Countermeasures
DERA	Defense Evaluation and Research Agency
DoD	Department of Defense
EO	Electro-Optical
ERAST	Environmental Research Aircraft and Sensor Technology
EW	Electronic Warfare
EWTES	Electronic Warfare Tactical Environmental Simulation
FLIR	Forward-Looking Infrared
FOAS	Future Offensive Air System
GCS	Ground Control Station
GDT	Ground Data Terminal
GIS	Geographic Information System
GMU	Guided Missile Unit
GNS	Guidance Navigation System
GPS	Global Positioning System
GSE	Ground Support Equipment
HAE	High Altitude Endurance
Halsol	High Altitude Solar
HARM	High-Speed Anti-Radiation Missile
HiMat	Highly Manoeuvrable Aircraft Technology
IFF	Information Friend of Foe
IFOR	Implementation Force
INS	Inertial Navigation System
IR	Infrared
IRLS	Infrared Line Scan
JBS	Joint Broadcast System
J-STARS	Joint Surveillance Target Attack Radar System
LAD	Landing Assist Device
LASS	Low Altitude Surveillance System
LOS	Lone Of Sight

LPI	Low Probability Intercept	
MAE	Medium Altitude Endurance	
MART	Mini-Avion de Reconnaissance Telepilote	
MASTACS	Manoeuvrability Augmentation System for Tactical Air Combat Simulation	
MATSS	Maritime Aerostat Tracking and Surveillance System	
MAVUS	Maritime VTOL UAV System	
MIT	Massachusetts Institute of Technology	
MLRS	Multipe Launch Rocket System	
MOSP	Multi-mission Optronic Stabilized Payload	
MPS	Mission Planning Station	
NAS	Naval Air Station	
NASA	National Air and Space Agency	
NASP	National Aero Space Plane	
NATO	North Atlantic Treaty Organization	
NAWCWD	Naval Air Warfare Center Weapons Division	
NOLO	No Live Operator	
NRL	Naval Research Laboratory	
OTH	Over The Horizon	
PLO	Palastine Liberation Organization	
RAE	Royal Aircraft Establishment	
RAF	Royal Air Force	
RATO	Rocket-Assisted Take-Off	
RFC	Royal Flying Corps	
RPV	Remote Piloted Vehicle	
RS	Reconnaissance Squadron	
SAC	Strategic Air Command	
SAM	Surface-to-Air Missile	
SAR	Synthetic Aperture Radar	
SATCOM	Satellite Communications	

	(Military)
SAU	Special Air Unit
SEAD	Supression of Enemy Air Defenses
SEAL	Sea and Land (Commando)
SHAAFT	Supersonic/Hypersonic Attack Aircraft
SPA	Special Purposes Aircraft
STAG	Special Task Air Group
TAC	Tactical Air Command
TBM	Theater Ballistic Missile
TIS	Thermal Imaging System
TML	Truck Mounted Launcher
UAV	Unmanned (Uninhabited) Aerial Vehicle
UCAV	Unmanned Combat Aerial Vehicle
UHF	Ultra High Frequency
UN	United Nations
UNPROFOR	United Nations Protection Force
URAV	Unmanned Reconnaissance Aerial Vehicle
USAAF	United States Army Air Force
USAF	United States Air Force
USCG	United States Coast Guard
USS	United States Ship
UTA	Unmanned (Uninhabited) Tactical Aircraft
VTOL	Vertical Take-Off and Landing
VTOR	Vertical Take-Off and Recovery

ACKNOWLEDGEMENTS

Thanks to:
Maj Gen K Israel
Rear Admiral B Strong

Authors:
Edward Lanchbery, 'Against the Sun'
Bill Wagner, 'Lightning Bugs and Other Reconnaissance Drones', 'Fireflies and other UAVs'
Richard A. Botzum, '50 Years of Target Drone Aircraft'
Curtis Peebles, 'Dark Eagles'
Hanna Reitsch, 'The Sky My Kingdom'

Individuals:
Richard T Wagaman
Julia Holloway
Jennifer Baer-Reidhardt
Dr D Harari
Norm Sakamoto
John Dale
Mark Day
Harry Berman
Dave Manley
Mark Sumich
Thomas J. Cassidy
Chris Haws
Ivan Rendall
Rick Spurway
Mike Greywitt
Renate Hulme
Barbara Tewwdt
Takahiro Kawada
Marvin Kelmow
Jocelyne Gallas
James H Christner
Patrick Chenieve
H Schriver
Gilles Laflamme
Sherrie S Shaw
Terry Timms
Wing Commander Russell Torbet
Michael Hartwig
C Panot
Charles Jacobus
Jan Svobda
Hal Klopper
Arthur Oates
Mike Lombardi
Jennie Hentger
Roger Smart
Heather Cox
Karen Engelbret
Doron Suslik
Annie Dijkstra
Dave Phillips
Mike Ryan
Bob Stuck

Companies:
AAI Corp

Aerospatiale Missiles
AeroVironment Inc
Alliant Techsystems Inc
AVPRO
AUVSI
BAI Aerosystems Inc
Bell Helicopter Textron
Boeing Defense & Aerospace Group
CAC Systems SA
Canadair
Cobham plc
Daewoo Heavy Indusrtires
DARO
DARPA
DRA
DERA
Deutshe Aerospace
Dornier GmbH
Eurodrone
Flight Refuelling Ltd
Freewing Aircraft Corp
GEC-Marconi
General Atomics Aeronautical Systems Inc
GIAT Industries
Israel Aircraft Industries/Malat
JPO
Kamov Company
Kawada Industries
Kentron/Denel
Lockheed Martin
Massachusetts Institute of Technology
Matra Defence
McDonnell Douglas Aerospace
McDonnell Douglas Helicopter Systems
Meggitt Target Systems
Metero Costuzion
NRL
National Archives
Naval Air Warfare Center Weapons Division
Northrop Grumman
Oerlikon Contraves
OmnipolThomson-CSF
Tracor IncTRW Avionics Inc
Teledyne Ryan Aeronautical
Tupelov OKB
Sagem SA
STN Altas Elektronik
Schweizer Aircraft Inc
Yakovlev OKB

Photography:
NASA
National Archives
RART
A P Bishop
Emil Buehler Naval Aviation Library
Nigel Easterway
Tim Gerlach
Denny Lombard
Mike Lombardi
Arthur Pearcy
Max Reid
Istvan Toperczer
Bill Young
Simon Watson
Maxwell White